Woman's Best Friend

women writers on the
dogs in their lives

———— ⟞⟟ ————

edited by
Megan McMorris

foreword by
Pam Houston

Seal Press

Woman's Best Friend
Women Writers on the Dogs in Their Lives

A version of Rebecca Skloot's essay, "The Truth about Cops and Dogs," originally appeared in *New York* magazine in October 2004.

A version of Sara Corbett's essay, "Running with Trout," originally appeared in *Runner's World* magazine in January 2005.

"Surrogate Dog" is excerpted from *Pack of Two* by Caroline Knapp, copyright © 1998 by Caroline Knapp. Used by permission of The Dial Press/Den Publishing, a division of Random House, Inc.

Some photos and illustrations are used by permission and are the property of the original copyright owners.

Published by
Seal Press
A member of the Perseus Books Group
1700 4th Street
Berkeley, CA 94710

9 8 7 6 5

Library of Congress Cataloging-in-Publication Data

Woman's best friend : women writers on the dogs in their lives / [edited by] Megan McMorris.
p. cm.
ISBN-13: 978-1-58005-163-7
ISBN-10: 1-58005-163-4
1. Dogs--United States—Anecdotes. 2. Women dog owners--United States—Anecdotes. 3. Women authors, American—Anecdotes. 4. Human-animal relationships—United States—Anecdotes. I. McMorris, Megan.
SF426.2.W65 2006
636.7—dc22
2005037675

Cover and interior design by Domini Dragoone
Printed in Canada by Transcontinental
Distributed by Publishers Group West

For Corvus and Otie

Contents

A Year Without Dogs
Pam Houston

We were put on Earth to be educated. I'm convinced of it. The Universe has a plan to make sure we don't ever stop learning, not only in our minds, but also in our hearts.

Nearly a year ago, my novel *Sight Hound* was released. It is the story of Dante, an Irish wolfhound, very like my own Irish wolfhound (coincidentally, also named Dante) who was and remains the one great love of my life. Dante (in the book and in real life) was diagnosed with bone cancer on his fourth birthday. Chemotherapy and an amputation earned him three more years—the three best years anyone could ask for—before the cancer came out of remission and took his life. Dante lived with grace and died with dignity, and touched—changed—more lives in his seven years on the planet than some people do in seventy. No one's life was changed more than mine, as Dante parceled out lesson after lesson, as quickly and as many as his recalcitrant, resistant, and eventually grateful student could take.

Dante taught me that if your paws are too big to fit in your ears, you have to get someone else to do the scratching, and that if you want your hand to be licked, you might have to put it under somebody's nose. He taught me that sitting in the grass together doing nothing isn't really doing nothing at all, and that sometimes, even if you haven't acted perfectly, the good thing happens anyway. He taught me that if you really love somebody, cleaning their bodily excretions off the carpet is no problem, and in the end, the money doesn't really matter a bit. He taught me that loving, in the face of inevitable loss, is the single most important challenge of our lives; that without loss, life isn't worth a hill of beans, and without love, life is nothing more than a series of losses. He taught me that everything is forgivable, that every moment contains eternity, and that loving unconditionally doesn't mean you are a self-annihilating fool. After he died he taught me how to live without him, but also that I didn't have to. He taught me that because we loved each other so completely, a part of him would always be with me.

My novel sold a lot of copies, which led to my giving a lot of talks and readings, 157, to be exact, and more are scheduled down the road. I have flown 90,000 miles this year, domestically, on United (not to mention the other carriers), which ought to be against some kind of law. I have been through airport security so many times that I can probably set a land speed record for undressing. I am thrilled with the response to *Sight Hound* . . . who wouldn't be? But the success of the novel has been inversely proportional to the time I have gotten to spend with my four living wolfhounds—Tegan, Fenton, Mary Ellen, and Rose—and because the time I get to spend with my wolfhounds is directly proportional to my sanity, 2005 has left me feeling more than a little insane.

I have spent the last year with wonderful strangers, dog people from every corner of this country who want to tell me their stories. They have shown up at readings in North Carolina and Alaska and St. Louis and Albuquerque with letters and photos. They have filled my inbox and my mailbox with stories of Utah and Bosco and Tripper and Archibald, the dogs that found them when they were ready to change their lives. I have sat up in hotel rooms reading these stories, crying quietly while SportsCenter or The Weather Channel drones on in the background, missing Fenton and Tegan and Rose and Mary Ellen, missing the big man Dante most of all.

My father—my last living relative—died in February. My

marriage, which has spent the last several years amicably dissolving, has finally entirely dissolved. The traveling I've done this year has taken away mornings at my friends' kitchen tables, it has taken away the comfort of my favorite sushi bar, my favorite bike ride, my favorite Peet's Coffee & Tea, my favorite hikes with my favorite hounds. Sometimes, at the end of a long trip, I take the long-term parking shuttle out to where my car has been sitting for ten or twenty or thirty days, and when I get behind the wheel I weep from the relief of my car's familiarity.

I know that this year, my dogs are better off without me. They have spent the time on my ranch with my ex, who adores them. They have each other, 120 wild acres to play on, horse poop to eat, rabbits to chase. No amount of wishing is going to squeeze an Irish wolfhound into a carry-on bag. They miss me. Especially Fenton, the little boy who so takes after his Uncle Dante, but there is no doubt that the dog who has taken this year's separation the hardest is me.

It is Thanksgiving morning, and for the first time since September, for only the third time this year, I am spending several days in a row at the ranch with my dogs. The Broncos are on television, the turkey is in the oven, and there are six hundred pounds of dog in the living room. Tegan is on the bagel bed, Rose is on the throw rug, and Fenton and Mary Ellen are butt-to-butt on the big yellow couch. It is sunny and warm by 9,000-feet-above-sea-level standards, and there is no reason that the dogs should be inside on a day like today. But mom is home for a change, and we all took a walk up Shallow Creek this morning, and now no one is about to let her out of their sight.

Rose, Fenton, and Mary Ellen

My friend Gary is here with the dogs and me for Thanksgiving. He lives across the country from me and is as busy as I am, but somehow we have carved out this peaceful week. I call him *my friend Gary* not to be coy, but because that is what he has been for twenty years. This past summer we slid into more-than-friend status. When our coupling doesn't seem highly insane, it seems perfectly natural. Most of the time it seems highly insane. I loved Gary a lot as a friend, and now I love him in so many other ways too, I can hardly stand it. This is the first time I have been afraid to lose anything since I lost Dante, and now, when it really matters, I seem to have forgotten everything Dante taught me. I can feel this big love cracking me open. I don't know what to do with myself.

Gary and I have a lot of fights, and usually it is me who starts them. They are about all the things that don't matter at all: ex-girlfriends and poorly worded emails and why he hates to talk on the phone. After the knock-down drag-out we had on Tuesday, Gary said, "Pam, the defense has been on the field now for a long time."

"Aren't the humans perfectly marvelous creatures?" Dante whispers in my ear, the way he does when he's hanging around near my left shoulder, "How they use all those highly developed language skills to drive away the very things they love the most?"

Some of our fights can be chalked up to being friends for so long that we are capable of saying anything to each other, and we do, without allowing for the particular sensitivities of new love. And there are the pressures of long distance. But I suspect the real reason I keep fighting with Gary is that I haven't had my dogs around to remind me how to love him; how to just be happy at the very sight of him; how to not take things personally (that he doesn't know how to send flowers, that he sometimes goes into the bathroom with the newspaper, and forgets, for an hour, to come out); how to remember the good things (like when he sang "You Can Close Your Eyes" to my voicemail when I was having trouble sleeping); and forget the bad things (see, I've forgotten them already); how to have faith that if we get through today, tomorrow we'll have even more time to go out in the yard and throw the ball.

We are sitting at the kitchen table across from each other, and gold Thanksgiving light is streaming in through the windows. Behind us, Fenton and Mary Ellen are snoring in unison on the couch.

Gary tells me his dead mother is speaking from the grave, telling him to be gentle.

I tell him my dead dog has his head on my left shoulder, telling me to be brave.

We should be okay as long as nobody overhears us, except the dogs, who don't pay any attention, because they've known this stuff all along.

———————— ⌁———⌁ ————————

I have no doubt that my Dante was the *greatest dog that ever lived*. I have no doubt that Sage, Tanny, and so many of the other dogs whose stories fill these pages are also the *greatest dogs that ever lived*. I have no doubt that you, too, the person holding this book in her hands, have known such a dog. How lucky we are to live in a world where almost everywhere we look we see another *greatest dog that ever lived*.

There's a line in a Stephen Dunn poem I love that goes, *Did you know that a good dog in your house can make you more thoughtful, even more moral?* I know it's true, and so do the women who wrote these essays. Abigail Thomas lets her dogs Rosie, Harry, and Carolina teach her that sometimes going outside at 5 AM is enough to banish melancholy. Katie Arnold lets the neighborhood stray she calls Hyena teach her that sometimes attachment is "so glacially slow it's indecipherable, little more than an instinctive stirring that escalates into something much bigger when you're not paying attention." After her sister gets diagnosed with inflammatory breast cancer, Abby Mims lets her mother's high-maintenance pug named Wally teach her how to move forward tentatively, "carefully reaching toward a place where we can start to believe again that the people we love are safe." And Julia Fulton (in an essay that makes me cry every time I read it) lets her dog Sage (rhymes with Taj) teach her how to survive earthquakes, how to keep her promises, and eventually, how to sit still and let herself be loved.

Dogs change lives. Half Buddha, half Bozo, they keep us tethered to the earth, and they teach us to fly. Our dogs are our sanity keepers. They are our suicide-prevention task force. (There I'd be with the gun in my hand, and Fenton would look at me and say, "What the hell do you think you're doing?" and of course he'd be right, as always.) They are the worthy and willing recipients of our fierce, unrelenting, and unconditional love. They are our personal trainers, our gurus, our reason to get up in the morning, our bed-warmers, our muses, our teachers, our hearts.

Dog Moms Are
a Special Breed
Megan McMorris

The collection you hold in your hands is the brainchild of my editor at Seal Press, Jill Rothenberg. It all began one day last January: I was minding my own business when an email popped up from her, asking if I would be interested in heading up this project. Hmmm . . . assign and edit stories about women and their dogs? Let's just say that no one had to twist my arm to sign up.

Jill's emails turned into phone calls, and then a funny thing happened: our calls gave way to long chats on Friday afternoons, when we both had a little more time to talk. Over the course of many friendly phone calls, our conversations spilled over into other areas of our lives: races we were running, birthday parties we were having, new boyfriends, ex-boyfriends, and yes, the trials and tribulations of our dogs. In more than five years of freelancing full-time, it was the first time I'd had this type of chatty relationship with an editor, especially with someone I had never met in person. It's not really that surprising though: Our mutual dog-mom status gave us an instant familiarity, a spark of friendship that led us into deeper conversations.

That's because dog moms are a special breed, which is something we wanted to celebrate with this book. We agreed from the start that we wanted stories that went beyond the clichéd, me-and-my-dog cutesy route. Instead, our goal was to compile a range of well-written stories about the many ways in which dogs affect our lives, both good and bad and somewhere in between. Armed with that mission, we went our separate ways and spread the word to every female-writer-with-a-dog we knew or knew of.

Luckily, our networking paid off in the form of these twenty-six stories (and one fabulous introduction from Pam Houston) about all realms of dogginess. We discovered that we have as many different relationships with dogs as there are breeds—from a Great Dane who doesn't live up to her breed's identity as a gentle giant, to a dachshund who takes up residence in the family car, to the many colorful personalities in between: two other dachshunds, four hounds, four Irish wolfhounds, three border collie mixes, two weimaraners, two yellow Labs, one golden retriever, one chocolate

Lab, one pug, one corgi, one keeshond, one greyhound, one husky, one Beardy mix, plus four mixes of various spaniel/retriever/shepherd combos, one undetermined mix of breeds, and one that, well, most closely resembles a hyena.

From short, humorous stories to longer, more poignant tales, the essays you find here all show the love—and yes, sometimes the love-hate—relationships we have with the dogs in our lives. They may be called Man's Best Friend, but as these stories show, there's truly no gender divide when it comes to our canine companions.

Thanks for reading.

Megan McMorris
January 2006

The Dog Whisperer
Abby Mims

When I come downstairs in the morning, my mother is falling apart. She is on her hands and knees in the living room, sobbing and scrubbing at the mess on the carpet that her pug, Wally, has left behind. Her nerves are beyond raw these days, and she is not sleeping—most nights I hear her pad quietly upstairs into the guest bedroom at three or four in the morning, where she listens to spiritual lectures on tape until dawn. She is forgetting things as well, sometimes asking me the same question two or three times in a day.

She keeps scrubbing, and I stand frozen for a moment at the edge of the carpet, not knowing what to do. Nothing unnerves me more than watching my mother fall apart. It doesn't happen very often, but when it does she is so lost that I am left unmoored, unable to hold onto the person I have always depended on. It leaves me feeling, in the most concrete of ways, that the world makes no sense. As I stand there, I realize that I haven't seen her like this in years, fourteen to be exact, the last time I lived at home.

Six months ago, my younger sister Kari was healthy and I was living in Hollywood, finishing graduate school and trying to become a writer, worrying mainly about agents, publishing, and how much traffic there was on the 405. Now, my twenty-eight-year-old sister is battling inflammatory breast cancer, and I am living back in the suburbs of Portland, Oregon, in the house where I grew up, trying to negotiate daily life with my mother, my stepfather, and Wally. Now I worry about MRIs and bone scans, and the difference between a Stage IIIC and a Stage IV diagnosis.

Something I didn't know about breast cancer before: Early detection is great and all, but no matter how many times you lie on your back with your arm above your head, feeling for pea-size masses, it is never as simple as finding the lump, getting it out, and slapping on a pink ribbon. Especially not when you have a rare form of the disease that makes up less than 1 percent of the cases, when the sneaky creep has moved to your lymph nodes and skin in less than two months, or when your tumor measures 10.5 cm x 3.5 cm x 9.5 cm.

"It's about the size of an ice cream sandwich," my sister said early on in this whole mess, as if we were all puzzling over this particular issue. "I've been thinking about it, and you could say it's something like a squished grapefruit, but that's not quite right." The two of us were standing in the kitchen when she had this revelation, and she opened the freezer and pulled an ice cream sandwich out to demonstrate. We'd bought a box of them the week before, because she can eat all the sugar she wants on chemo days. She held it up to her breast and made a circle in the air around it with her index finger. "You see?" And I nodded, wanting to snatch that harmless rectangle from her hand, toss it outside into the late fall sun, and watch it melt to nothing.

I move toward my mother now, sit down on the couch, and ask her what's wrong. I assume that all the scrubbing and crying has to do with what Kari has endured—and will endure—in the coming months: chemo, a possible mastectomy, more chemo, radiation, removal of her ovaries, premature menopause. But she tells me no, that isn't it, this meltdown isn't about Kari.

It's about Wally. It's about the dog.

"It's very depressing to have a dog that barfs all the time," she says when she catches her breath. Among many other things— he barks at the ceiling for no apparent reason, he refuses to go for walks unless most of the family is going, he obsessively licks his own nose when he feels insecure—Wally has terrible situational anxiety. This causes him to throw up when other dogs are around, when he goes somewhere new, when he knows he's going to be left behind, and sometimes, most times, for no reason at all. He has a sensitive stomach, my mother says. An easy gag reflex. She has even gone so far as to develop a scale of intensity to normalize

Wally

this behavior. For instance, if he's only done it once in a day, this is not so bad, or if he's gotten into the cat food or the garbage, anything that isn't his special vet-prescribed dog food, this simply doesn't count. This behavior has been going on since he was a puppy, but it has gotten steadily worse since my sister got sick, and my mother is starting to take it personally.

"Everyone is always telling me what to do about it," she says, leaving the spot on the carpet for a moment and sitting up to face me. "Like I haven't tried everything, like I don't know what I'm doing, like I'm a horrible dog mother."

"Mom," I say, trying to reel her back in, "no one is accusing you of that, no one thinks that." She shakes her head and goes back to her scrubbing. "He was weaned too early, that's all. He's got issues." I want to believe this is true, that some kind of Freudian complex drives Wally's various neuroses, but I know dogs tend to respond to energy and often reflect the emotional states of the people around them. Essentially, if Wally's calibrations are anywhere near accurate, we are all something of a mess.

Dogs have a long history in our family, big ones mostly, Labs and retrievers. They have been around since I can remember, even going back as far as the night I was born—when my mother was in labor, my father was rescuing my aunt's retriever, Crazy, from the middle of a frozen lake in Montana. Growing up, we had a black Lab named Quentin, who, by the time we could ride on his back or curl up against his stomach, was a fat, lazy beast. He was around until I was eight, when my parents divorced and we had to move into an apartment complex that didn't take dogs. He went to live with my aunt and uncle then, on several acres north of Seattle. We visited him in the summers, and the August he was dying, my sister and I sat in the barn with him every night after dinner. I kept his head in my lap and Kari rubbed his silky ears and we both pretended not to notice how slow his breathing had gotten or the effort it took for him to pull air into his lungs.

A few years later, when we moved into a house again, my mother brought home a hyperactive cocker spaniel that promptly ran smack into the sliding glass door, knocking it out onto the deck. He then turned around and bit my mother and was never heard from again. A few weeks later she brought home Oreo, a Lab/retriever mix who wasn't so smart and was more than a little codependent—she had a hard time going anywhere without my mother. I was a teenager and my mother loved this new dog, and therefore I couldn't stand her. Looking back, that dog was everything she needed at the time: a peaceful, dependent being who offered unconditional love and comfort when at least one of her children was providing her anything but. Oreo was thirteen when she died, and it took my mother several years to recover, but when she did, she decided what she wanted was a small dog with a big dog personality. A dog that could walk with her and sit in her lap, offer her extra company when she needed it, and serve as a substitute for the grandchildren that were nowhere in sight. That's when Wally arrived, as a two-pound puppy you could hold in your palm. Sweet, tiny, and, we would soon discover, incredibly high maintenance.

------------------🐾------------------

Kari is living near Bainbridge Island while she goes through treatment in Seattle, and my parents and I alternate staying with her for a week or two at a time. Wally comes less often, nervous as he is, but when my sister is a few sessions into her first round of chemo, my mother brings him for a visit. Kari's face has taken

on a slightly waxy appearance by then, and her hair has started
to fall out in the most disturbing of ways—not in clumps, as one
would expect, but instead via a gradual thinning process that has
made my beautiful sister look something like an old man with a
receding hairline. She is fond of making me scream and flinch by
lifting up the layer of hair that is left and exposing the bare skull
underneath. It is a reaction she never tires of, one that I am starting
to understand gives her some kind of pure, twisted joy. In a few
more weeks, she will shave her head, as she will no longer be able
to tolerate waking up to a pillow full of hair. For now, she wears
scarves and hats. She hates the wigs we've gotten for her.

If you ask, she will say she is fine, she is doing fine, and all
the attention and bustle around her isn't necessary. She is tired,
though, and she looks it, and my mother is doing her best not
to worry, but her mouth involuntarily becomes a thin, tight line
whenever my sister catches her eye. There is nothing my mother
hates more than when she is accused of being anxious or overly
concerned, and I think this is why she holds her breath longer
than the rest of us do each time Wally is brought into a potentially
stressful situation. We all do it, really; we wait and cross our
fingers, hoping that this time he will leave behind all of his
insecurities and fears and develop a new approach to life. In fact,
we all did it two days ago when he arrived, yet the puking has

hardly abated since, no matter the amount of hand-wringing, soft coos of encouragement, or denial my mother employs to cope.

"He hasn't thrown up all morning," she says. "You see? He's getting better."

"Mom," I say. "He threw up ten minutes ago."

"That wasn't anything," she says. "It was hardly anything, anyway." Other things my mother does to combat their mutual angst: She hums Hindu mantras designed to dissipate all things worrisome and insists on keeping the dog practically strapped to her side at all times.

This is how Wally ends up in the back seat of the car on a trip to the grocery store one day—we have just gotten home from chemo and we need something, a protein powder or oat bran or one of the two dozen supplements the naturopath says my sister should be taking to counteract the side effects of treatment. My sister says she wants to go with my mom and Wally to the store because she is stubborn and strong-willed, and because she will say she is fine. This won't change as the months go on, as no matter what she is going through or how much it hurts, she will endure and manage to keep it together to the point that the rest of us will end up looking like pathetic, deflated shadows of our former selves.

I am standing on the back porch, contemplating whether or not to water the plants there, when the car pulls back into the driveway. I walk around to the front and find the passenger door open, my sister nowhere to be found, and my mother looking genuinely panicked. They have been gone less than five minutes.

"Shit, shit, shit," she says. "Everywhere, it's fucking everywhere. Help me, would you?"

And it is everywhere, on the upholstery, the doors, the floor, the ceiling. I am halfway into the car with wet rags and Wally is backing himself into a corner, trying to avoid his own mess, when my sister walks slowly up the driveway. She is drained of color and when she reaches the car, she puts her hands on her knees, bends over, takes off her hat, and lets her balding head dangle.

"Jesus," she says, "Jesus, I can't fucking do this." Then she slowly stands back up and walks toward the house. I hand my mother a rag, meet her eyes. We both know Kari is talking about more than cleaning up after the dog, and it is unnerving to see her like this, overwhelmed and fragile, actually acting like a cancer patient. My mother looks back down at the upholstery and we don't say anything to one another; we just wipe and clean and scrub until there is nothing more we can do.

Things only get worse after this incident—my sister's treatment trudges on, we all (particularly our mother) grow more tired and anxious, and the dog responds in kind. By the time my sister is recovering from surgery in Portland, it's gone way beyond throwing up—he now barks nonstop outside the door while my mother tries to meditate, he follows her around and attacks the vacuum when she cleans, he yips at the ceiling when she isn't paying enough attention to him, he runs in circles around the couch where my sister tries to sleep. My mother is cracking under the pressure and has started to talk about finding Wally a new home.

"I can get him to stop all of it," Kari says from the couch. It is only a few days after her lumpectomy and she is sore and bruised, her rib cage and chest still bound tightly in bandages. A tube runs from the bottom of the bandages to a plastic receptacle, one of the drains she has to keep in for a week that will do the work of the lymph nodes she had removed in the surgery, pushing out the waste her body is producing. She pushes herself up to a sitting position, wincing a little. "It's all about being calm and assertive at the same time."

"Really," our mother says. "How so?"

What she does not know is that in the past few weeks, my sister has discovered a man named Caesar who has a show called *The Dog Whisperer* on the National Geographic Channel. He has become my sister's newest fascination, her focus really, and his genius and techniques are most of what she wants to talk about these days, instead of how she feels or what we can do to help or what the next phase of her treatment is going to be. She insists I watch with her two or three times a week, and I do have to admit that he pulls off nothing less than miracles in canine behavioral modification.

"You have to act like the mother would in the wild. Or like the leader of the pack. No bargaining, just instinct, orders, and response," Kari says.

"But I don't want to be mean," our mother says. We both roll our eyes. Our mother never wants to be mean. "And nothing we've done until now helps anyway, not the trainer or the walking schedule. Nothing. Plus, honey, I think you've got other things to deal with at the moment."

"It's fine," my sister says, "because I can get him to stop from right here on this couch. I swear to God."

My mother acquiesces, and Wally begins his training. He spends five days on a short leash next to Kari in the TV room, and she sits there radiating calm assertiveness, never raising her voice or yanking on his collar when he tries to bolt or starts to bark. Much like Caesar, she makes a low, sharp noise from between her teeth and flicks the leash enough to let him know that his behavior is not acceptable. After the first few hours of this routine, he is less agitated, and by the third or fourth day, he is turning to look at her before he makes a move to do anything.

Over the next few months, Kari continues her dog-whispering routine with Wally and he miraculously barks and barfs less. It even appears that the overall spectrum of his neuroses begins to narrow. Around the same time, we all are allowed to exhale slightly when the pathology from her surgery comes back cancer free, she gets through her second round of chemo, and the color starts to come back into her face. My mother starts sleeping through the night, and I stop obsessing (for at least a few hours at a time) that my sister is going to die.

It is not over yet, however, and there will be scares down the road, like the new lump she will find in her breast when she starts radiation or the masses on her ovaries that will materialize before her second surgery. In those moments, before we know it is only so much fatty tissue and a couple of harmless cysts, any footing we've gained will suddenly be lost and we will be right back where we started, the panic rising in our throats and the familiar sharp dread poking at the bottom of our ribs. We will all try to follow Kari's lead when these things happen, to take in some of the calm she projects and try to keep breathing. For a long time, though, we will all act a little like Wally still does when he meets new people or visits unfamiliar places. He puts his nose out timidly and sniffs, and although he may retreat at first, he is slowly, slowly getting brave enough to move forward and rub up against the unknown without panicking to the point of losing his lunch. Like him, we are all moving forward tentatively these days, carefully reaching toward a place where we can start to believe again that the people we love are safe.

Little Dog, Big Heart

Susan Cheever

I was brought up to believe that there were two kinds of dog people. Big-dog people were smart, classy, generous, whiskey drinkers. They didn't hug and kiss each other; instead they relied on shoulder punches and handshakes to express affection. Small-dog people lived in over-decorated apartments, where they talked about their needs in screechy voices and drank only sherry. Cat people were not even discussed.

I was proud to be a big-dog person. Our household was crowded with shambling, oversized retrievers. The myth was that we had dogs because they were useful—although none of our family Labradors had ever dreamed of actually retrieving a bird. We were not the kind of family who would have had dogs who loved us extravagantly; any talk about a desire to be loved was definitely frowned on. In our family, love was complicated, beset with rules and regulations, and often a source of embarrassment.

Our dogs were gorgeous creatures with silky coats, fluid movements, and deep, liquid eyes. They came from breeders with WASPy names who lived in large clapboard country houses. These breeders had silver martini shakers and shared our distaste for small dogs and our contempt for pet shops and puppy mills. Our dogs seemed to like us well enough, but they weren't passionate about it. After all, they had come from generations of aristocrats so who could blame them for being standoffish? We gave them elaborate show-offy names like Cassiopeia, after the Ethiopian Queen whose constellation edges the summer sky in New England, and Ezekiel, after a 17th-century ancestor named Ezekiel Cheever, and Flora MacDonald, after the nurse who fled from England with Bonnie Prince Charlie.

So how did I end up with a miniature dachshund named Cutie? How can I love a passionate, shrieky little critter whose idea of work is to find a patch of sunlight and curl up in it, or to burrow under a pile of quilts with just a tiny tail sticking out? Isn't it canine heresy for me to harbor a lap dog whose entire thirteen pounds is devoted to expressing love, needy love, unmannerly love, blatantly embarrassing love? Sure, dachshunds were bred to hunt badgers. Cutie has never seen a badger, and his idea of a badger hole is a sleeping bag with my son inside.

My disintegration happened slowly. As an adult, at first I had my own retrievers, but I went for golden retrievers, the friendlier kind. Maybe I was hungry for a little affection. I certainly wouldn't have admitted that. Then when the time came to buy a dog for my daughter, we scouted hundreds of types of dogs and settled on a Pembroke Welsh Corgi—a big dog in an apartment-sized body, perfect for our Manhattan lifestyle. Our corgi was named Lydia Hutchinson after an obscure New England judge. She came from a country house kennel, Roughhouse, and the day we picked her up the deal was sealed with a lunchtime martini.

Lydia was elderly by the time I decided to buy a dog for my son's ninth birthday. We were living in a medium-sized apartment, but the rooms often felt too small for the playing and working and milling around that went on there. When my son said he wanted a golden retriever, my heart sank. Then one night at a dinner party, the host's miniature dachshund, Melvin, hopped up on the chair next to my son. My son looked over. Melvin's whiskers twitched. He put his little black nose under my son's arm and gave it a push so that he would embrace him. The deal was done.

The day we went shopping for a dachshund was the day I learned that shopping for a dog means buying a dog. At the pet store, the salesman put us in a room with a three-pound ball of black and tan fur. The ball of fur latched its tiny arms around my son's neck and began to lick his face.

"His name is Cutie!" my son said with a huge grin.

"We're not even sure we're getting him," I protested. "Why don't we go get some lunch and think it over?" I hadn't intended to buy a pet shop dog; I wasn't sure about a dachshund. I have often thought that people look like their dogs. I imagined my beautiful children growing into dwarf-legged, pointy-nosed clowns, and I said it again. "Let's leave him here and think it over. We can come back." Both children turned to me in disbelief. "Why don't we name him Rilke," I said, "since dachshunds are German. Or Goethe?" No one heard me. Soon Cutie, wrapped in a purple sweater, was in my son's arms, while I wrote out a check with many numbers on it.

Cutie

What is it like to break the mold? Fortunately Cutie turns all serious questions into good humor. It's hard not to smile around Cutie. There is something about him—his long body and short legs, his expectant face, his proudly lifted little tail, his inquisitive, perked-up ears—that makes me laugh no matter what else is going on. We like to joke that Cutie has a PhD from the University of Cuteness—I even designed a little diploma for him from the *Universitatis Cutensis.* Like many dogs, he's a natural comic, signaling dinnertime like a whirling dervish, but he's all business when it's time to go out for a walk. Cutie the dachshund is a mind-altering drug.

Cutie doesn't just love unconditionally, he positively vibrates with enthusiasm. When he sees someone he loves, his tail wags and his whole body wags with it. Every furry molecule seems to radiate gladness. He lets out howls of exuberant joy. Cutie doesn't care if I have eaten an extra cookie, or if I have missed a deadline, or if I am a bad mother, or the kind of shopper who likes to think things over. He loves the essential me, the person I know is in there even when I'm snapping at my children, or criticizing a friend, or weeping with frustration over a paragraph that won't get written.

When Cutie was three and had won our hearts, his back began to hurt him. He stopped jumping. Then one day he couldn't walk and we rushed him to the Animal Medical Center. The surgeon told us that his back problem was probably caused by a ruptured disc. He would need a myelogram and surgery as soon as possible. The cost would be around $3,000, the surgeon said. She said it was good that he had only lost the use of his legs a few hours earlier.

Cutie looked very unhappy about all this; my son expressed *his* feelings by slumping to the examination room floor and sobbing. For a second I actually wondered if it was alright for me to spend thousands of dollars and days of time on a thirteen-pound animal when many people in the world don't have places to live or enough to eat.

Cutie had the surgery and a long, painful recovery. I was up with him many nights, stroking him and telling him that he would walk again although the doctors were not so sure. I learned to help him by supporting his back legs, giving him massages and hydrotherapy, and trying to encourage him to urinate, a sign that his organs were working again.

Facing a tiny, sad body on the newspaper-covered floor of the bathroom at 3 AM, I experienced my own dachshund night of the soul.

"Do animals have souls?" I asked a friend.

"I'm not even sure that *people* have souls," he told me.

Back in the 1960's I worked in the civil rights movement, and I spent one long summer tutoring on a college campus near Montgomery, Alabama. There were dogs everywhere on campus, scavenging outside the cafeteria, living under the dorms, and owned by no one. Late one homesick afternoon I saw a roly-poly yellow puppy start across one of the campus roads and get hit by a car. The puppy screamed and limped away; the driver shrugged his shoulders and drove on. I scooped up this puppy and tried to comfort it. People stared at me. I walked to the local hospital cradling the bleeding dog in a town where hatred would soon lead to murder. I have never felt quite as out of place in the world as I did in those minutes. I finally got there and found a man I knew from the college. Since I already had dogs of my own, I begged him to take care of the little thing that had fallen quiet in my arms. He said he would; I knew he wouldn't. I let him take the dog anyway.

In the six years since Cutie has joined our family, I have become increasingly haunted by our treatment of the animals in our lives, from the painful, cruelly designed lives of the veal calves who end up as our scaloppine, to the groomed, cashmere-swathed bichons frises of the Upper East Side. I have become a vegetarian. I avoid buying leather. What does it mean to own a living creature? What responsibilities does that entail? What are our obligations to creatures we encounter like the puppy in Alabama?

Many wise people have written about what we can learn from animals. Cutie doesn't seem concerned about the questions his presence poses for me. All he wants is to have his back scratched so that he can flip over with his legs in the air and have his stomach rubbed. His pleasures are simple and complete: a walk on a warm day, welcoming my son when he comes home after school, dinner, hearing a few kind words, the occasional biscuit. His great talent is knowing how to love. I hope I have learned something about that too.

Sooner or Later:
Your Dharma

Dimity McDowell

Four years ago, my husband, Grant, and I moved from a Brooklyn brownstone to a Santa Fe adobe and adopted Dharma, a two-year-old weimaraner. It never occurred to me to change her name. I liked that she wasn't a Bailey or a Jake or a Daisy. Plus, she had distinctive features—ears that turned light pink when the sun hit them, a tail that was chopped too ambitiously, and a delicate scar on her back right leg that marked where she'd been hit by a car—and she deserved her distinctive name. On a walk when somebody asked me her name, I replied, "Dharma, like the television show *Dharma and Greg*." I usually got an odd look in response, but I dismissed the questioner as a brainy type who prided herself on not owning a television.

What I didn't realize—and what the interrogator definitely

35

knew, as a resident of Santa Fe, where crystals and negative energy fields are discussed more often than the weather—is that "Dharma" is a Buddhist word that means the principle or law that orders the universe. My next-door neighbor, who has long gray hair and an overflowing heart, explained the concept when she gave me a bumper sticker that read SOONER OR LATER: YOUR DHARMA. Or, in other words, my destiny isn't in my hands. I wasn't sure if the canine Dharma was my actual Dharma, sent via the Weimaraner Rescue Society, but I decided to go local and embrace the New Age thing. I gave Dharma the benefit of the doubt and listened—or "opened my heart," in Santa Fe–speak—to what message she had for me.

Like all guiding principles worth paying attention to, Dharma came on quietly. Her demands were minimal. She didn't eat for the first forty-eight hours after we brought her home. She happily accepted her bed on the floor and didn't whimper for the couch or our bed. While I worked at home, she slept at my feet, and when I got up to go to the bathroom, she'd follow me and, sensing my modesty, dutifully sit in the doorway with her nose facing out. On hikes she was painfully shy. When another dog approached on the trail, she'd carve a U-shaped detour through the surrounding brush to both avoid the dog and meet back up with me. Giving her affection was near impossible; in addition to her aforementioned

scar, her cowardly nature and her habit of flinching whenever
anybody approached made it clear her previous owner had abused
her. I had to pet her on her back and neck before I touched her
head. Grant had it worse: It took over six months until she'd let
him touch her.

Even so, within days I loved her more than I thought I'd
love anyone whose poop I had to pick up. Whenever I walked in
the door, whether I'd been gone for hours or was just bringing
in a second load of groceries, she'd circle around me and wag
her stub of a tail frantically, as if she'd thought she'd never see
me again. She could hear the crack of a banana peel from rooms
away and, once given a bite, would chew laboriously, as if she
was eating rawhide. On walks, when we came upon a lush lawn,
a rarity in arid Santa Fe, she'd nosedive into it, like she was
jumping into a lake. At night, she resisted the urge to fall asleep
so badly—she was, of course, trying to stay present—her eyelids
fluttered for minutes before she finally succumbed. I adored all
that and more.

Despite her low-maintenance personality, Dharma
started to assert her presence almost immediately. Grant and
I, the stereotypical couple who uses a dog as a test-drive for a
potential baby, learned the usual lessons: how to compromise ("I
walked her yesterday," I'd whine in the morning, "so today I get

to stay in bed"); how to covet unconditional love; how to always request plastic bags over paper at the grocery store. But any dog can teach you those things. I wanted more from Dharma, whose intense yellow eyes and silky, monochromatic gray fur gave her the sophistication of an old soul who'd seen it all. I was looking for answers to epic questions: What is the purpose of my life?

Dharma

Why does suffering exist? How can I be at peace? Baby steps, she replied. Her first order of business, being a Buddhist messenger, was introducing me to a more Spartan lifestyle. In other words, she destroyed most of the material possessions I had lying around the house.

Her first lesson involved a one-of-a-kind purse, bought in Brooklyn, which stood as a symbol of urban hipness in my new city, where turquoise and leather fringe decorate way too many accessories. While I was out for a morning run, I left the purse at her eye level and she chomped into one of its perfectly faded royal blue straps. I salvaged it by cutting the other strap to the new, shorter length and safety-pinning both of them to the purse, and I didn't discipline Dharma. I didn't catch her in the act and therefore couldn't punish her—one tenet of dog discipline

I'd heard again and again—nor did I have enough insight to realize that there were similar teachings soon to come.

Sensing what was essential and what was expendable, Dharma wisely stayed away from big-ticket items like couches and rugs. She rarely ruined anything outright to get her point across. Instead of using gashing chomps, she'd make tiny, fishlike bites that slowly eroded an item, much like grains of sand carve canyons over years. And she'd do just enough damage to remind me of her presence: My jean jacket now has one buttonhole that no longer holds a button.

Over the next three years, as Dharma nibbled her way through $3,000 worth of goods—a conservative estimate—I tried to channel my anger over my dwindling wardrobe into understanding how, if this Dharma was my universal guiding principle, what it all meant. It wasn't always easy. I saw no reason for her to shred three backpacks, since I'd already learned the safety-pin lesson (read: Be adaptable) with my purse. When she attacked my beloved olive green down jacket on three separate occasions, I got down on my hands and knees to gather all the goose feathers and patched it. Lesson: Sometimes love is hard work.

Rendering four television remotes unusable was easy to interpret—watch less, think more—as were the ripped pockets in a handful of fleece jackets—don't tempt unnecessarily, or more specifically, don't leave Milk-Bones in the pockets—but holes in two pairs of running shorts and in a pair of dressy wool trousers were more difficult. Was she telling me to wear more jeans? Pulling the stuffing out of Grant's thirty-year-old teddy bear, one of his few remaining pieces from his childhood, was an unnecessary, harsh reminder not to hold onto the past.

It took the mangling of several pairs of sunglasses and regular glasses, including Grant's Giorgio Armani frames, before we learned to reconsider what we previously thought was unnecessary—insurance, in this instance—might not always be. My cashmere sweater, one of my loosely classified upscale items, suddenly had a diagonal tear across the chest when I left both it and Dharma alone momentarily on the bed one morning. Teaching: Don't trust unconditionally. The destruction, during one particularly costly episode, of a down comforter, duvet cover, and foam mattress pad could be interpreted in only one distinctly non-Buddhist way: payback. One year into living with us, Dharma, without an invite, upgraded from her bed to ours. Every night around midnight, she'd slink up to our bed, then slam all seventy pounds of her into me. When my spine couldn't take it anymore, I began to kick her off the bed as soon as she crept up. Lesson: Remember karma or pay the consequences. If she couldn't sleep in comfort, neither could we.

But nothing matched her penchant for ankle-high athletic socks, of which I admittedly had a surplus. Weimaraners are bred to be hunting dogs, but on walks, Dharma couldn't have cared less about rabbits or other varmints. Instead, she turned her keen seek-and-destroy instinct on socks. The first time she ate one—and I didn't know she had until I was on pooper-scooper duty—I fretted about the effect it would have on her constitution, but then realized it had handled the journey easily. She's eaten so many at this point that when I see a singleton in my drawer, I don't assume I've lost it in the laundry, I assume it's lost in Dharma's intestines. When something goes wrong, I reflect on the fate of the now-divorced socks and remind myself of Dharma's sock-nibbling lesson: This too shall pass.

Dharma took her socks whole but her leashes bit by bit. She ruined them, I think, to lead by example—her possessions numbered two bowls, one for food, one for water; and her bed, which was too precious to destroy—so leashes were the only expendable items in her immediate universe. After she neatly divided an expensive leather leash into three bits and halved a pink-and-brown grosgrain ribbon one, bought at a fancy L.A. boutique because it perfectly complemented her fur, I moved on to generic, cheap styles. Evidently price was not an issue for her, as she made her way through those too. She chewed leashes when she was left in the car, when she was tied up to a post, when I foolishly left them on a table. I finally wised up but, given Santa Fe's leash laws, couldn't heed her lesson: If you love somebody, set them free. Her current, fourteenth leash is homemade out of recycled climbing rope, and I store it on the top of a seven-foot-high rack.

Most rational (read: less enlightened) people might ask why we allow her to continue to roam free when we leave the house. Truth is, after we discovered her nibbling tendencies, we tried several strategies to stop the havoc. Our initial idea was to lock her in my office, which I cleared of anything savory, or so I thought. When we returned, she'd mangled the telephone wire box and doorknob so badly we had to replace both. Lesson: Notice the details. So we bought a giant crate, thinking that, with time, she'd adjust to having her own predetermined space. Wrong again. She tore apart the towels and sheets that lined the crate and ripped her "friends," one-dollar stuffed animals from the Salvation Army, to pieces. There was so much stuffing when we returned home that her crate looked as if it was riding on a fluffy cloud of spun polyester. The only time she really slaughtered teddy bears in a rabid, bare-her-teeth way was when she was captive, and when she started hurting herself by chewing on the crate, causing massive bleeding sores on her inner lip, we knew we had to free her.

After all, the abuse she had endured in her earlier days had been more than enough for a lifetime. Buddhist or not, even I could appreciate that concept.

So instead, we instituted a new verb—"Dharma-proof," which means clean off every surface, close every door, put away anything that might be juicy—and we now do our best to Dharma-proof the house every time we leave. But we often miss something and even when we don't, she surprises us by expanding her range to things like jars of Vaseline or tubes of toothpaste. Every time I return home, I hold my breath until, Dharma at my heels, I've done a quick run-through of the house. Lately, though, I've been neglecting my Dharma-proofing duties. She's only caused minor destruction over the last year—namely, one rain jacket and one cotton sweater—so I think she knows I'm now ready for step two toward my Dharma. I sincerely hope it doesn't involve material goods this time, but—like a good student—my heart is, of course, open to anything.

Puppy Hater

Robin Troy

My boyfriend, Mike, calls me a puppy hater. Not exactly the first two words I'd hope someone would use to describe me, but after this first Year of Molly, I admit I can't deny the charge. Again and again I've tried—I was raised with three golden retrievers; how could I hate puppies? What kind of person hates puppies?—but fresh from mopping up Molly's most recent nervous pee, I think the best I can do is qualify it.

There are some puppies that, under certain circumstances, I just don't love right off the bat. And to me, Molly isn't just a puppy. She is a time-suck that I did not choose. She is a border collie mix from the pound that Mike picked up on a whim. At a time when he was a full-time student running his own company. At a time when he already had a nine-year-old hound named

Jesse. At a time when he and I were talking about moving in together after three years of a relationship in which my biggest beef went like this:

"I feel like every decision in this relationship is dictated by Jesse, or now Molly, or Jesse and Molly, or Molly and Jesse—never Robin and Mike."

The night I met Mike, I had been living in Missoula, Montana, for two weeks. Mike had been there for ten years. He lived in a small cinder block house in an alley behind a pizza place. Jesse found her snacks in the dumpster and slept in Mike's bed. She had previously been owned by a hunter who had decided after one year that she was a useless hunting companion, and his solution was to shoot her. Mike saved her. He lovingly nicknamed her various drools—the wraparound drool, the unidrool, the debris drool—and showed off how she broke into a reflexive howl, even in her sleep, at the single strain of a Dylan tune. She belonged on *Letterman*, Mike said. She was his princess. Definitely, she was his first love. He said he would have her cloned before she died.

Until then, though, Jesse would call the shots. For me and Mike there would be no hiking or running on trails where dogs weren't allowed, or where they must be leashed. No listening to Bob Dylan in the car with Jesse because her howling continued long after the charm had worn off. No leaving her alone in the house during the day because her barking would attract the cops, responding to the neighbor's noise complaints. No leaving her alone at night because she'd get into the trash. No letting her get too close to unfamiliar dogs or small children because you could never guarantee that she wouldn't snap at them. No getting a good night's sleep at Mike's place because there'd be twigs and hound hairs in the bed. No sleeping two nights in a row at my place because Jesse would be lonely.

"But she's a *dog*," I'd say.

"But she'll get lonely," he'd say.

"But all she does is sleep at night."

"I just hate to think of her being lonely," he'd say. "I wish she had a—"

Enter Molly. Mike first brought her to my house when my father was visiting, so I had no choice but to smile. My dad liked her; Mike was smitten; I didn't want to be the grinch. But I have to admit that in my first moment looking at Molly, at that squirmy, unconditional bundle of love, all I could see in her needy black eyes were the reflections of me and Mike, ten years down the road, still dealing with this whim.

More immediately, we would need to negotiate puppy training into our already-delicate Jesse schedule. Now there would be no hiking or running on dog-friendly-only trails for more than a mile or two, so as not to tire the puppy, and all such runs and hikes for the foreseeable future would be disrupted by efforts to make Molly learn to sit, stay, come, lie down, heel. Forget adult conversation: Mike now used the same voice to call both me and Molly "baby." There would be no more sleeping at Robin's house, no more walking shoeless on Mike's piddle-riddled floor, and plenty of griping about how classes and jobs and now no backyard at Mike's new apartment—none of which were secrets before his trip to the pound—didn't leave enough time to take care of two dogs.

Molly and Jesse

And then, naturally, Mike had to have surgery. It was my first day at a new job, Molly's fifth week in our lives. For a week, Mike was conked out on his couch while I drove back and forth from work to his apartment every two hours to juggle his prescriptions, quiet the dogs, feed the dogs, walk the dogs, wipe up Molly's pee, clean up Jesse's shredded garbage, Lysol the floor, assuage the neighbors, and repeat. At the end of the week, Mike said it was the first time he could imagine me as a mother. Funny, because for me it was the first time I could imagine myself as a puppy hater.

But I should pause here. I love Mike. From the first day, I loved Jesse. And I'm not ruling out that someday I'll love Molly, too. For their litany of petty inconveniences, Jesse and Molly have also been integral to the happiest times in our relationship: climbing mountains, swimming rivers, meeting people who wouldn't have stopped to talk to us if we hadn't been with Jesse and Molly. When I am honest with myself, I admit that my frustration with Mike's dogs is that they show me a part of myself I don't like. I am not a patient person. I am tightly wound. I need order. I look at Jesse and Molly and see a part of Mike I envy. Unlike me, he has a reservoir of calm that allows him to make time and room for these animals for which he clearly does not have time or room. Our different responses to his dogs illustrate how opposite our personalities can be. And since opposites do what they do, here we are, three years into a relationship that neither one of us sees ending. Which is why, when I got a job in Connecticut, Mike agreed to make the move—and, for the first time, move in—with me.

Bless him. Because not only is Connecticut no Montana, East Coasters are no Montanans, either, and the cost of living is far from that of two-dollar Big Sky pints and eighty-nine-cent movie rentals. Where Missoulians are likely to have a litter of mutts in their pickups or loose at their sides, the East Coasters we've witnessed so far have a single, groomed poodle in their Beemers or behind an electric fence.

Thus, any of the roughly one hundred phone calls I made to find us a place to rent either went like this:

"Do you take dogs?"

"No."

Or this:

"Do you take dogs?"

"How many?"

"Two."

"No."

Or this:

"Do you take dogs?"

"How many?"

"Two."

"What kind?"

"A hound and—"

"No."

Or this:

"Do you take dogs?"

"How many?"

"Two."

"What kind?"

"A hound dog and a border collie mix."

Pause. Then reluctantly, "Yeah, okay. But there's a $500 pet deposit and a $100 monthly charge per dog. The carpet's old and the last renters broke the screen door. Drive by first and see what you think. Call back if you're still interested."

I never was. What I was interested in was the long list of ads for clean, affordable rentals that did not accept pets. I was interested in silencing the snicker that came through the phone each time I gave another landlord our price range and pet status. I was interested in how different my life would be if Mike didn't have dogs.

"They're your dogs now, too," he'd say to me.

"No they're not," I'd say.

"Don't worry," he'd say, which is what he always says. And as usual, he was right. A couple of weeks into rental-hunting, my miracle arrived in the form of an MBA student who withdrew from school at the last minute—the same minute I poked my head into his realtor's office—and lost his deposit on a cozy, affordable, beachside cottage *that would allow pets*. I stood on what would soon be our new deck and called Mike, who was back in Montana putting his faith in me to find us a place, and told him we'd been saved. There was just one catch: The realtor told me she was only going to write one dog on the lease.

"But we have two dogs," I told her.

"I know, but I just think it's better if I write down one."

"So you're saying that if there are two dogs I shouldn't tell you?"

She nodded.

I agreed. I told Mike we would pretend to have one dog.

"Sure," he said, unfazed. What did he care about a white lie on a lease all the way across the country? As I spoke, he was palling around with friends in Missoula on a sunny June day, Jesse at his side. Only Jesse looked a little funny, he said. She looked bloated.

"Is she okay?" I asked.

"She seems tired," he said.

"Call me later," I said, and I drove to my parents' house an hour from our new home. At ten o'clock Mike called. He was crying. He told me Jesse was dead.

"*What?*"

"Dead," he said.

Then silence.

My first thought was that I'd killed her. Hours earlier, I'd signed a lease for only one dog. I'd even told the broker that Jesse was old, that she might not live much longer. She was ten. The vet told Mike her organs had failed. He'd taken her to be looked at and was told to put her to sleep on the spot; she was filling up with fluid, and her heart couldn't beat fast enough to keep her on her feet.

My second thought was that this wasn't fair—Mike hadn't had a chance to clone Jesse. That black, heart-shaped splotch on her back, those seal-pup eyes, those long ears Mike used to wipe the drool from her jowls, or clean the gunk from her eyes. Mike had not had an adult life without her. The first time I'd kissed Mike we'd been outside his cinder block house behind that pizza place, Jesse wedged between us.

On the phone that night, I cried as much as Mike did. Sure, we could both rationalize that Jesse's spirit belonged in Montana, not Connecticut—we could practically hear every electric-fenced, purebred homeowner within a ten-mile radius of our cottage breathing a sigh of relief. But for us, losing Jesse was shocking. For Mike, it was a life chapter closing. For me, it was the first time Jesse felt like my dog, too.

I flew back to Montana to pack, and Mike and I sprinkled Jesse's ashes on top of one of her favorite peaks. The container from the vet wasn't filled with ash so much as small pieces of bone. Jesse looked like bits of coral. A week later, two days before I left Montana for good, I climbed the same peak without Mike, and the pieces of Jesse were still there on the bald summit. Not even those high, dry winds had budged her.

But Jesse had always been a stubborn beast. And while it's hard to say that sometimes even sad things happen for a reason, the truth is that life in Connecticut with Jesse would have been tough. Life in Connecticut—in a heat wave, with no A/C, with all the humidity and traffic and *very important people* that Montana blissfully lacked—started out tough enough. But when Mike arrived one week behind me with Molly and his U-Haul, things got tougher still.

The first night went like this: Mike pulled into the driveway at 4:30 AM, exhausted. I stumbled from bed, half asleep. He suggested tying Molly to the back deck. I told him I'd seen a skunk there earlier in the day and had been listening to an animal rustle under the deck all night. Mike tied Molly to the back deck. Ten seconds later, Molly got sprayed by the skunk. Mike let Molly in the house. The house I'd spent all week cleaning stunk. I got mad at Mike. He got mad at me. Welcome to our new life.

The details aren't novel. Dirty paws on the carpet, claws through the screen doors, food snagged off the counter, tufts of black hair everywhere, whining and barking and every other messy Molly behavior I'd already witnessed when Molly was just Mike's dog, living in Mike's place. But in one fateful swoop, she'd become my dog, too, in our place, and none of my mental preparation—*Be calm, Robin, don't worry, carpets are just carpets*—

carried me through those first days with any grace. I snipped at Mike. I yelled at Molly. I was a control freak without control, a Type A poster child saddled with a bachelor and a puppy, a neatnik living by a muddy, sandy beach.

My parents came up the first weekend for a picnic. To my surprise, they offered to pile all of us, including skunky Molly, into their clean car to drive to a bigger beach ten miles away. When Molly leapt from the way-back into the back seat, disrupting all the picnic bags and landing in my lap, my parents didn't flinch. They laughed.

At the beach, my dad couldn't wait to take Molly for a walk. My mom burst into hysterical laughter as Molly dug holes at our feet, spraying sand all over our food. Mike and my parents were dying to see if Molly would swim. She'd never been to the beach before. I'd never had a wet-and-sandy Molly racing through our house before—and I hated myself for letting the thought in.

Lucky for me, Molly wouldn't budge. My dad coaxed, Mike wheedled, but Molly wouldn't go near the breaking surf. Instead, she planted herself under our umbrella, digging holes while my parents delighted in her and Mike and I soaked up our happiest afternoon since we'd said goodbye to Montana.

My mother called the next day to say she'd been tickled by Molly. She and my dad had laughed the whole drive home, she said, telling stories about her. In the background, my dad asked if we'd tried to get Molly in the water again.

"She'll get in," I heard him say.

"She's a good dog," my mom said.

Are you guys for real? I thought. I hung up and tried to understand how my parents could relish the one part of my relationship with Mike that I thought might break us. It took me a while, but I think I figured it out.

My parents embraced Molly because they have been living with each other, sharing their space and idiosyncrasies, for over thirty years. What's another spot of mud on the carpet? When their golden retrievers were Molly's age, my mom and dad were in their twenties, younger than I am now. They were newly married, first-time homeowners, and I was on the way. It was arguably one of the best points of their lives—of any life, for that matter—this point that I am closing in on now. With Mike. And Molly. And really, the challenge is not that I'm a puppy hater. It is that I am a person learning to share my life with another living being. That being is not a dog. He is Mike. And neither one of us has done this before.

Mike and I took Molly back to the big beach the next day, and each day thereafter. Each day, she dug in her heels far from the water, and each day Mike—and soon I—became more determined to teach her to swim. We would stand in the water calling for her, clapping, begging, telling her what a brave girl she was. Once, Mike carried her in, only to have her scramble to the dunes. We tried kneeling in the surf, sitting at the water's edge, digging primitive sand-castle moats, all to lure her closer.

When those tactics failed, we turned our backs. We swam away from Molly and stood in the water, our arms around each other. We faced the sea and looked at how far we'd come. Montana was a world away, and I think a part of both of us was itching to click our wet heels and be home. For now, though, *this* was our home. Our first one together. It was an acknowledgment worth hanging onto, and so I slunk down in the water, level with the horizon, and wrapped my legs around Mike's waist. He pulled me to him and kissed me. And Molly went bananas. From shore, she howled. She slapped at the foamy water and ran from it. She couldn't stand to be left out. She barked and whined, and when we wouldn't budge—when we held our ground, holding on to each other—Molly took a running leap over the breaking surf and into the water.

You should have seen us: We cheered like crazy people. We leapt out of our skin. We waved and splashed and Molly hung in there. She swam for Mike, and I swam away from him, and then she swam for me. And there's no taking that moment away: Molly's dainty face, her timid paws, those bright black eyes yearning for nothing more in that instant than to reach me. I would have given her anything in the world right then. I brought her into my arms, and she clawed through the skin on my legs, and then she high-tailed it back to shore. It was a quick first swim—a thirty-second victory in a strange new time—but it was a beginning.

The Hyena at the Door
Katie Arnold

I don't remember when he first showed up. One day he wasn't there, the next he was, roaming the streets on the edge of darkness, a shadowy blur of fur. He fit right in with the countless other feral animals stalking my Santa Fe neighborhood: mangy rottweilers on rattly chains, free-range chows, squirrel-size Chihuahuas yipping at car tires, rogue mongrels with scarred snouts and dark personalities camped out on street corners. The only thing that set him apart was how spectacularly awful he looked—eighty pounds of matted, overgrown fur, ribs poking through like toothpicks, teepee-shaped ears plastered to an emaciated face. In the early days, sightings were so rare that when you saw him streaking by, it was like catching a glimpse of a wild animal—the elusive beast of Rodriguez Street.

"He looks like a hyena," I told my boyfriend, Steve, as we crossed paths with him one cold, rainy night about three years ago. His eyes glinted alien green in our headlights, and his sloping back arched in a defensive recoil. He was part predator, part prey. He looked half drowned and vaguely dangerous.

We named him out of habit. There were so many oddball characters running around our neighborhood, we needed a way to keep track of them all. In our lexicon of nicknames, the Chihuahua who flirted with death was Road Pancake (until it vanished), the snowy husky mix that lived down the street was, unimaginatively, Whitey, and the woman across the arroyo who cackled loudly at her TV was Laugh Track. Even my own dog, a chocolate Lab named Gus who occasionally answered to Peanut, was not exempt. It was only logical that the shaggy, wild-eyed stray of undetermined age, gender, and pedigree would henceforth be known as the Hyena.

Before long, the Hyena had set up a de facto butcher shop in the weedy scrub between my house and garage. Licked-clean bones started littering the yard. He didn't discriminate: skinny chicken wings, gopher skeletons, decaying rabbit carcasses, every sort of beef bone imaginable, discolored meat hanging off them in strings. Aesthetically speaking, it was a disaster—Serengeti slaughter meets the local landfill—but the neighborhood isn't exactly pristine.

Junked cars on blocks and boats that haven't floated in years are scattered about with careless abandon, prime targets for the nonexistent Neighborhood Beautification Committee. Unsightly as it was, the Hyena's butcher shop was not out of place.

Gus was a regular customer. He'd make his evening rounds—checking the Hyena's inventory, cleaning up scraps—then come home and puke up chalky bits of bone all night.

I worried about nameless disease. "Do you think he's going to get sick?" I asked Steve, sopping up the puddle of barf with a paper towel.

"He *is* sick," said Steve. He was talking about the half-starving Hyena. I was talking about Gus.

It wasn't long before the Hyena began supplementing his diet with delicacies poached from nearby trash cans. Looking out the bedroom window, I'd survey the remains of his last meal: empty KFC buckets, still-greasy McDonald's french fry envelopes, family-size lard containers, soggy posole bags, sushi containers (wasabi and fake grass intact), cans of tuna and black beans, and—what appeared to be his personal favorite—dozens of takeout ketchup containers, squeezed down to a sticky nothing. Some days I cleaned up after him; other days I didn't. I resented the inconvenience of his mess, the intestinal havoc it wreaked on Gus. Maybe he'll just go away, I hoped, and take his trash with him.

He didn't.

A faint path began to announce itself, trampled grass and pawprinted dirt leading from the butcher shop to a cluster of juniper bushes in the no-man's-land between my property and my neighbor's. The Hyena's base camp. The trail cut kitty-corner across the yard, joined the flagstone path along the porch, then looped

Hyena

down into the steep arroyo, where Whitey kept a snug doghouse and a frequently replenished bowl of chow. For as long as I'd lived there, the sandy wash had served as a veritable stray highway, offering safe off-street passage, the shelter of several forsaken vehicles, and—thanks to Whitey's stash—free food and water.

Soon my property was crisscrossed with Hyena migration routes. From the fleecey comfort of his designer dog bed in the kitchen, Gus had a clear view of his nocturnal wanderings, and the Hyena proved to be a creature of habit: Each night at approximately midnight, he ventured out to his scavenging grounds. I knew this because each night at approximately midnight, Gus sounded a ferocious murderer-at-the-door alarm. And each night, jolted from sleep, I cursed the wretched Hyena.

My relationship with the Hyena was complicated from the start, an uneasy blend of resentment, denial, and guilt. I didn't love him for a lot of reasons. He was trashy and skittish and untrustworthy. His skulking around made me uneasy. I already had a dog, who I loved with a fierce single-mindedness that bordered on obsession. Gus, as far as I could tell, was peerless in every way: glossy and well groomed, cheerful, perfectly adjusted. Any behavioral deviance—including, but not limited to, scrounging for bones—I blamed entirely on the Hyena. Another dog would require affection, and all of mine belonged, rightfully so, to Gus.

But most of all, I didn't love the Hyena because I felt guilty. I'd committed an act of unthinkable treachery that had doomed him to a life of misery.

The incident occurred on a sleeting winter day, a few weeks before I first noticed him. I was home alone when a woman rang my doorbell. She was jumpy and wet and wasn't wearing a jacket. Her story was hard to follow: She was "borrowing" a friend's dog, and somehow it had escaped. Had I seen it? She didn't live in the neighborhood, and she didn't have a phone, but her friend did. She provided a vague description of the dog—big, long brownish-blond hair—and produced a phone number on a crumpled scrap of paper. Standing in my doorway and looking past me into my living room, she made me nervous. I was suddenly convinced this was a scam, that at that very moment someone was jimmying my back door to steal my stereo. Technically, that wasn't possible—my back door was in plain view of my front door—but something wasn't right.

I took the number and assured her I'd look for the dog, then promptly locked the door behind her. In the time it took me to case the place for intruders, I convinced myself the dog didn't exist. The paper stayed on my kitchen counter, only because I didn't get around to throwing it out. I never looked for the dog, nor did I think about looking for the dog. Not long after, I ran into my neighbor at the mailbox, who asked if a strange woman had come to my door looking for a dog. The way she said it made it sound like she didn't believe her, either. When I got home, I chucked the number.

A couple weeks later the Hyena, a scrawny heap of dirty fur, lurched out of the shadows and into my guilty conscience. Karmically speaking, I knew I was in trouble. I tried to ignore him, but the butcher shop was becoming an eyesore, my otherwise congenial Gus was channeling his inner Doberman, and every time I caught sight of the Hyena, I'd feel a prickly stab of shame. He was evidence of my inner badness, and I wanted him gone.

So began my amateur dog-catching campaign.

The Hyena wore tags, barely visible under his mane of fur. They were his ticket home. I didn't relish the idea of a close encounter with his fleabag coat and wizened canines, but I needn't have worried: He wouldn't let me get within fifty feet of him without tucking his tail, bawling, and bolting in the opposite direction. Raw hot dogs, launched from my bedroom window, did nothing to gain his trust. I baited my backyard with bacon, then left the gate open, hoping he'd be lured in (although I hadn't thought through what I'd actually do with a caged Hyena). No luck. Clearly, he was afraid of humans, impervious to the temptations of pork.

Steve watched from the sidelines, an amused but unwilling accomplice. He's a garden designer, one of those strong, silent, earthy types who makes his living tending to living creatures; plants thrive under his watch and animals flock to him. Several months earlier, an errant Chihuahua had shot out of nowhere, raced up his leg, and clawed at his knee in a surprise micro-embrace. Ever since, Steve had been fantasizing about getting a second dog: a pint-size Chiwi that he could tuck into his jacket while he backcountry-skied or stow—along with his tabby cat, Hazel—in the front basket of his bicycle. Short of that, I knew he'd settle for the Hyena.

But that wasn't part of my plan. I summoned the dogcatcher. "There's a big stray dog around my property," I told the dispatcher the first time I called. "He's scared and I think he could be mean. I'm not sure I want to catch him myself," I said, neglecting to mention that I'd tried, and failed, on several occasions.

"Don't approach the animal. Just keep it in the area until the officer arrives," the dispatcher replied, neglecting to explain how to do one but not the other. Fortunately for the Hyena, unfortunately for me, my neighborhood is a medieval maze of alleys, dead ends, and dirt lanes; illogical street addresses only confuse matters. My house would burn to the ground before the fire truck ever found it. Even the local animal control officer, who cruises the neighborhood with his dog prong and torture-chamber truck on a far-too-regular basis, was never able to locate it. After half a dozen tries, I gave up and gave in. I made a deal with myself, and the Hyena: I wouldn't necessarily help him, but I wouldn't hunt him down. Whether he stayed or left was up to him.

Attachment is weirdly unpredictable. Sometimes it's immediate and transparent: five-week-old Gus, a chocolate ball of puppy love, hurling himself at my ankles. Other times it's so glacially slow it's indecipherable, little more than an instinctive stirring that escalates into something much bigger when you're not paying attention.

Once I stopped stalking the Hyena, an odd thing happened: I stopped worrying about his trash heaps. I no longer felt guilty that, thanks to me, he was a homeless scavenger while my own purebred dog ate premium food from a stoneware bowl. Somewhere along the line, my resentment toward the Hyena turned into ambivalence, which, at roughly the speed of winter yielding to spring, gave way to acceptance.

In matters of the heart, I take my time. I'm a champion at hedging my bets. Defending against sudden disappointments is my standard operating procedure—even if it means warding off something far more profound and powerful, like actual joy. Steve had been around longer than the Hyena, yet in some ways his status was just as ambiguous. He had a key to my place and practically lived there, but he still commuted to his house each morning for a change of clothes before heading to work. It was a sore subject. When he'd raise the matter every six months or so, I'd dodge it, convinced that before he moved in, I needed answers to every question about our future. Steve didn't have the answers, but he gave me what he did have: patience.

In his own unhurried way, the Hyena was lobbying for residency, too. On winter nights, he'd creep into the garage or curl up not ten feet from the bedroom window, the heat from his body melting a forlorn little doughnut hole in the snow. He no longer fled the moment we approached. Instead, he'd back away slowly, mossy eyes unblinking. Sometimes he'd howl when he saw us: a high-pitched, conversational, almost owl-like *whoo-whoo*—his way of saying hello. We were starting to feel like one big happy family.

Then one day, after checking on the Hyena, Steve surprised me with some news. "Guess what? I think the Hyena's a she."

Our Hyena? Big, unruly, still slightly scary Hyena? It was like finding out that King Kong is really Queen Kong. You think you know someone, only to discover that your fundamental assumptions are all wrong.

Rattled, I reverted to my original strategy: The Hyena could sleep wherever *she* wanted, but I wasn't going to aid her cause. And I certainly wasn't going to feed her. I was sure that if I did, she'd become a pest, a beggar, a commitment I couldn't keep. That she'd move into the house and hijack my affection.

Or worse, she'd leave.

One day about six months later, I fed the Hyena. There was nothing particularly different about that day—she was as hungry and jittery as she'd been for three years—but a sudden urge came over me, and I knew it was time. "Hi, Hyena," I called out to her as I dumped a scoopful of Gus's kibble on the brick floor of the garage. Across the driveway, she cocked her head and watched. When I came out the next morning, the food was gone.

I'd violated my own rule, so I needed a new one: Feeding her was all right, just not regularly. And definitely not every day. My theory, ripped from the script of *Wild Kingdom*, was that if she came to depend on handouts, she'd forget how to forage for herself and lose whatever primal drive compelled her to sniff out fried-chicken grease and gnaw through Hefty bags for her supper. The rule suited me at first; I forgot about feeding her more than I remembered. Two scoops in the garage one day, half a scoop out by the butcher shop a couple days later. I kept both of us guessing.

It was Steve who mutinied. "Did you feed the Hyena today?" he asked one evening after he noticed her loitering by the front walk. She'd closed down the butcher shop in favor of a more domesticated approach to dining: begging.

I reminded him of my policy. "If we start feeding her regularly, where will it end?" I asked.

"Who knows?" he said. "But she's hungry, and you've already fed her once. Might as well keep doing it."

He was busy chopping vegetables for a stir fry while I sat on the kitchen stool, flipping through catalogs backwards. After four years together, we'd finally arrived at an understanding: Anything requiring sharp knives or precision—especially the slicing of onions, with all those tricky layers of skin and assorted bristly ends that might or might not be disposed of properly and might or might not accidentally wind up in the stir-fry itself—was Steve's domain. He had the cool confidence and experimental flair of someone who'd done time in professional kitchens. He didn't need or use recipes; he made them up as he went along, and they invariably turned out. I, on the other hand, was reckless and easily distracted, completely dependent on cookbooks, and generally unsuccessful. My specialty was dishwashing.

In the kitchen and out of it, Steve and I were natural complements to each other. I had only just begun to realize what he'd understood from the start: that our differences weren't a liability, and that true attachment didn't mean you had to find someone exactly like you. All the good things he had—calm, common sense, cooking expertise—were things I'd always wanted and needed, even when I didn't know it.

It was time to commit. It was time to buy the Hyena her own food.

In the pet aisle at Albertson's, the familiar guilt came rushing back. Could I really, in good conscience, feed the Hyena generic dog chow while Gus got the good stuff? I belabored the question for about thirty seconds, then settled on a cheap, small bag of the "savory" chicken-and-pea variety. To mark the occasion, I fished a scratched stainless steel bowl from my cupboard, filled it with kibble, and carried it out to the rusting Pontiac GTO parked beyond my front fence. The car, missing a wheel and the back windshield, sat on blocks beneath a cottonwood, high enough off the ground that the Hyena could wedge herself under the backseat passenger side where the muffler should have been. It was shady and cool— her summer camp. I placed the bowl on a small slab of flagstone, and called to her with a soft lispy whistle. Something rustled under the car, and the Hyena emerged with a yawn. Then she did something altogether new and shocking: She wagged her tail.

After that, Steve and I took turns feeding her—once, and before long, twice a day—on her flagstone plate out by the wrecked GTO. Steve had a thing for cracking raw eggs on top, to help shine up her coat. Soon her butterscotch fur was glossy, her long swooping tail as fluffy as a feather duster. Her ribs disappeared. She began to shed—thick tufts of hair fell off her in clumps, carpeted the garden, clung to cholla spines, and drifted on the breeze like raw cotton. One lone dreadlock hung from her right ear like a dangly earring. "She's a good-looking dog," Steve said, a hint of pride creeping into his voice. "But I'd sure like to brush her."

To brush her we'd have to touch her, so we began luring her to the front porch with dog biscuits. It wasn't hard. One treat—the color and scent of cardboard, tossed out on the floor—was all it took. Then there she was, nose to the screen, waiting for us to appear with another. Each time, it was more or less the same routine: I'd dangle the biscuit from my fingertips, and she'd spin around in an excited little circle and take two tiny ballet steps in my direction.

Tempted, I'd stretch my arm toward her, and she'd jerk backward. Her final move was part giraffe, part camel, and all instinct: Craning her neck for maximum extension, she'd peel back her lips and pluck it from my fingers with the tips of her front teeth. Before I could so much as graze her head with my hand, she was trotting off, biscuit sticking out of her mouth like a stubby cigar.

It wasn't pesky—it was cute.

Now I love the Hyena. Officially, and without reservation. She's just like our other pets, only she lives outside. She lies in the front yard, on a flattened patch of grass, waiting for me to come home from work. She wags at me when I give her treats and bows down on her elbows when Steve appears with an egg. On warm afternoons when I lie on the porch swing reading a book, Laugh Track laughing across the way, she and Gus stretch out on the steps, backs to each other, sniffing the air and sunbathing.

I still worry, only my concern comes in a different form now. I worry about her like she's mine. I worry about the coyotes that slip out of the arroyo at night and try to corner her, yipping maniacally until Steve yells out the window and scares them off. I worry about the dogcatcher nabbing her. And I worry about what will happen when she finally lets me pat her and I get a look at her tags. Then what? Will we have to send her home? And what if her real name is Tiffany?

But there's no point getting hung up on the details—things have a way of changing anyway. Not long ago, Steve asked me to marry him, and I said yes. Soon after, the Hyena finally shed her long last dreadlock, and her tags fell off. I could look for them in her dirt nest under the GTO, but I probably won't. It's okay not to know.

Just the other day, a designer who lives across the arroyo stopped by to talk about plans for an addition to our house—where the butcher shop used to be. As we stood in the weeds looking at the site, the Hyena loped out of the junipers and sat down beside us. "Don't worry, she's friendly," I reassured him. "She's just a stray who lives around here."

"Oh, I know her; she's nice," our neighbor said. "She comes by our house all the time."

A dull thud of disappointment knocked on my chest. All this time I had thought the Hyena was something that had happened only to us. She was ours.

But of course that's not the case. She belongs to everyone and no one. That's just the way it is.

Running with Trout
Sara Corbett

We named our dog months before we found her. It was a game my boyfriend, Mike, and I liked to play over time, as we morphed from kids dating into slightly older kids living together in a renovated barn in New Mexico. *If we got a dog, what would we name it?* This was somehow more comfortable than batting around names for the children we weren't yet certain we wanted to have, but nonetheless it was a quiet measure of our hopes. We were young. We didn't want to get married. We just wanted a dog. And chatting idly as we walked through a local farmers market one day, we hit upon the dog's name: Trout.

Our primary requirement for the imaginary Trout was that he or she be a runner. Mike and I ran five or six mornings a week before work, usually on one of the myriad trails that began in

Santa Fe's sandy valleys and climbed into the scrubby foothills of the Sangre de Cristo Mountains. Usually we ran separately and at different paces. Often we each ran with a friend or two. The point was we were runners and not walkers, and while we understood that dogs needed to be walked, we were clear on the fact that our Trout would run instead.

That winter, I took to browsing the chainlink kennels at the local animal shelter almost daily, often locking eyes with its forlorn inhabitants and wishing I was bigger-hearted or less choosy. But I wasn't. I could be ruthlessly dismissive. There were squat little terriers and nub-headed pit bull mixes, which, no matter how good natured they seemed, still struck me as decidedly too short legged for the job of being my dog. The German shepherds—abandoned ranch dogs, mostly—seemed too big to be regular runners, too heavy in their bones. The chow chows had so much fur. The spaniels seemed so spastic. And every so often my heart would break for the random toy poodle or Pekingese who surfaced at the shelter, looking dazed and confused, as if he'd just been drop-kicked out of a New York limo.

Then one day I came upon a batch of squirming new arrivals—three tiny pups who'd been discovered eating garbage on the north side of town, with no mother in sight. The shelter vet put them at six weeks old and surmised they were mostly

Labrador retriever, but "with something else mixed in." Slowly, I lifted one of the puppies from the pen. Her belly was bloated with worms. Her nose was running. But she had rich cinnamon fur and lively eyes and her tail, no bigger than my finger, wagged gleefully. She licked me squarely on the lips and then settled into the crook of my arm, as if to say, *Good. When do we get out of here?* It was that simple.

Trout was only four months old when she went for her first run. It was a short outing, a slow trot along a dried-up riverbed not far from our home. On the vet's advice, we limited our distance but not our enthusiasm: Trout scampered along next to me, occasionally darting into the sagebrush or pitching her tiny body over a fallen log. She was joyful and so was I. She'd race ahead, then charge back—my deliberately slow pace clearly vexing her puppy patience. But growing dogs can damage their ligaments with any sort of demanding exercise, and so Mike and I always cut those early runs short, herding her back inside the house so she could hit the water bowl and then curl up for a nap while we went on to finish our distance.

My parents, who flew out from Massachusetts to visit us, immediately saw Trout as family. Not only was she an exuberant pup, but they took her presence in our lives to be a long-awaited sign of maturity. If Mike and I could brush, feed, and exercise a dog, then maybe we were capable of getting married and producing grandchildren, rather than leading a life my mother often referred to, less than delicately, as "bohemian." Trout made us look suddenly promising. Our landlord, who had been initially reluctant to allow a dog, took one look at Trout's silky ears and hopeful expression and declared that she could stay

Trout Marie

forever. "But you're calling her Trout?" he said. "That's too masculine. She needs a middle name, a feminine one." He studied the dog another minute. "Marie," he said finally. "Trout Marie." And so she was.

Like people, dogs grow into runners over time. They develop a running style, a pace, a routine. Once Trout Marie was two years old and considered full grown, she started running in earnest. We'd rise in the early morning and drive to our favorite trail, where she'd bound up the side of a low mountain and then backtrack to find me, huffing my way up behind her. It became clear that the "something else" in Trout's mongrel blood made her a skillful runner. Unlike pedigreed labs, who develop barrel-shaped bodies and a loafing gait, Trout was leggy and narrow, her torso lean like a blade, her belly arched, her stride powerful and light. People guessed she might be part whippet, but the mysteries of her heritage would remain just that.

Every so often, Trout would opt for a mellow run, matching my stride with an even canter. Other times, she was pure animal, structuring her route solely on the scents carried on the breeze, disappearing for long stretches in the brush. We were far away from any roads, so I never worried. Also, Mike and I understood early that Trout would never run away. Her stint as a garbage-eating stray had taught her to forever appreciate a roof over her head and a nightly can of Alpo. When time was short, I ran along the road with Trout on leash, which required a two-way adjustment. Trout had to put up with staying by my side. I had to put up with the stop-and-start of her unceasing, territorial need to sniff and pee.

Then one fall, Mike and I picked up our bohemian lifestyle and moved it east, to rural Maine—with Trout, of course, in tow. There, we took meandering runs on hilly country roads. When we explored the rocky, pine-choked trails, Trout wore a blaze-orange dog vest so some hunter wouldn't confuse her for a deer. It wasn't until November arrived, though, that I understood how much I relied on Trout for motivation. The winds picked up, the rain started to fall. Then the rain started to freeze, and the wind didn't let up. The roads were slick with ice, the sky hung low, eternally flat and gray. As a native New Englander who'd spent the last seven years in more westerly climes, I'd forgotten about this stretch of the year—the miserable, lonely part that doesn't relent until late April. I tried to adapt. I'd make hot chocolate, put on a big woolly sweater, crank up the gas heat, and stay inside. But then there'd be a warm, wet nose nudging my elbow as I worked at the computer or read a book. Trout would lift her ears expectantly. *Come on now,* she seemed to say. *You owe this to me.*

People who own dogs like to talk about their constancy as friends. It's legendary stuff—the way dogs love their adopted humans, the deep well of compassion and trust you will find in the eyes of any well-cared-for canine. Doglike devotion, we like to call it. Cats don't have it. Hamsters, horses, fish, best friends, and lovers may have their merits, but it is arguably only a dog who puts you at the center of her universe and keeps you there for life, even as you sometimes fail her. There have been many cold winter days when I've put on my wicking long underwear, my polypro socks, my wind-stopper jacket and thick hat, clipped the leash to Trout's collar, and taken her out for a bracing, subzero run. And there have been plenty of other times when I've scratched her behind the ears, let her out into the backyard for twenty minutes, and promptly resumed my cozy spot in the chair. I'm human, after all. What Trout seemed to know intuitively, though, was exactly what I kept forgetting: Without fail, regardless of the conditions, running made us both happier souls.

The year after we moved to Maine, my mother, who was fifty-four, was killed in an accident. In a single instant, it was as if the oxygen had been sucked right out of our lives; the earth abruptly reversed its spin. Nothing seemed normal. Everything seemed cruel. Mike and I left our place in Maine and moved temporarily into my family home in Massachusetts, to help pass those first lonely nights with my father. Trout, whom my mother had doted upon, calling her "granddog," slept by the door to my parents' bedroom, partly as a show of solidarity with my dad and partly because I think she, like the rest of us, was still expecting my mom to show up. And yet it was only flower delivery men and neighbors bearing casseroles who came, ringing the doorbell incessantly. Trout snarled and barked ferociously—the only time I've seen her like this—perhaps thinking she could chase off the deep grief that was settling over the house. It didn't work, but I loved her for trying. The only bit of normalcy came in the late afternoons, when Trout and I would slip out for our run, traversing the hills in a nearby bird sanctuary. It was in those sweaty moments, listening to our shared footfall, that I felt her constancy most.

We got older. We got wiser. Mike and I surprised everyone

by getting married—nine years after meeting—on a Maine porch one foggy September day, surrounded by family and a handful of our closest friends, with five-year-old Trout snoozing at our feet, a garland of wildflowers around her neck. We bought a house in the small city of Portland. We had a baby. Not long after, we had a second baby. Sometimes we laugh at how average we've become, the happy cliché of having two kids, a house, and a dog. My mother might have willed it exactly this way.

The truth is that for Trout, life after children has been a mixed bag. She often has a toddler clambering over her, and there can be such mad chaos in the house in the evenings that she has to remind us, with a nudge of her nose, that she hasn't been fed. Back when there were just three of us, we were efficient, active, and calm. As a pack of five, we're dirtier, more erratic, less tame. For exercise, Mike and I carry little bodies up and down the stairs and pick toy trains off the playroom floor for the hundredth time. Sometimes we feel lucky just to reach the end of another day. Trout looks at us and sighs, deeply, as if to say, *How did we get this way?* Still, she doles out her affection in full, on-the-lips kisses and at night drapes herself on the floor alongside our bed, one ear cocked in the direction of the children's rooms, listening for the sound of someone needing comfort.

Early parenthood and serious running—as most anyone will

tell you—are at best a juggling act. At worst, you simply don't run much. One day I loaded our son into the baby jogger, which I pushed with one hand while holding Trout's leash with the other. Between her sniff-and-pee breaks and his abrupt decision to start screaming, "Out!" at the top of his lungs, we barely made it a mile. As we turned around and headed for home, I made a vow to myself that I'd never try to take them both running at the same time again. Give me a choice between dog and kid as a running companion, and I'll take the dog any day.

So we keep trying. A few times a week, I leave the children to Mike, and Trout Marie and I try to cook up some of the old magic on a running path not far from our house. These are not long runs. Trout is ten years old now, and her muscles get stiff after more than a few miles. When it's hot out, I leave her at home—she glares at me out the window as I leave—knowing that it can take hours for her to cool down. Her body's grown thicker, her face is rimmed with white fur. But she's still as gung ho as she was as a pup. I've lost plenty of running partners over the last years—to yoga classes, to demanding jobs, to hectic lives as parents—but I haven't yet lost Trout. Say the word "run," and she still leaps toward the door, tail wagging furiously. Running feels good. It breeds elation and a reliable sense of calm. Trout never forgets that. In this way, I'm trying to become more doglike in my approach to running—

more Pavlovian, if you will. I banish all thoughts of the work I didn't get done, the trip to the grocery store I won't make, the sleep I didn't get last night, my life's tight leash. I say, "Come on, old girl," speaking to myself as much as to Trout. Then I follow her to the door, and we set ourselves loose again.

Surviving Grete
Tish Hamilton

Even the most casual dog observer knows that Great Danes are supposed to be gentle giants.

Dog books claim that the well-bred variety is easygoing, lovable, and good-tempered. In the old days, Great Danes were bred to hunt wild boar and guard the castle, but today their cartoonish size is mostly played for laughs. Like Marmaduke and Scooby-Doo, they're goofy, bumbling, perhaps not the sharpest pup in the pen, but in the end thoughtful in their own big way. And mellow. Above all, mellow. Too bad no one told Grete.

My husband, Eric, and I debated the dog question for two years before we finally got a puppy. We agreed early, however, on what kind of dog we'd get. Why a Great Dane? Over the next decade we would get that question a lot. (And then, why two?

Why three? After a certain point, you just say, why not?) The simple answer was that my husband's sister had a Great Dane, Louise, whom we adored. With her tortoiseshell coat and easy way with small children, she was everything you'd hope for in a dog. Handsome, good-tempered, low-key. But the deeper, more idealistic answer was that we saw promise in a big, calm dog lying on the floor of a modest-but-respectable home in a nice neighborhood with good schools and low taxes, tolerating all that modern life throws at dogs, including babies scampering over her. We didn't even discuss it much. A Great Dane seemed perfect.

Two years later Eric got a job with odd hours. One of us would be home four days a week, which we thought was enough time to meet the demands of a puppy. Out on a long run, we decided to name our puppy Grete (pronounced Greta), after nine-time New York City Marathon–winner Grete Waitz. Not that she would run (Great Danes are too big for long distances), but we pictured riding as a trio to my husband's triathlons, saw me cheering on the sidelines, Grete by my side. Cool dog, people would say. I'd smile.

We should have known better as soon as we met her. She was called Tinkerbell at the time, and a more woefully inappropriate name for this dog was hard to imagine. She was black, with white legs, a white chest, and a white collar that didn't quite circle her neck, making her an imperfect "Boston," just short of show quality. Her ears had been clipped (not our choice) and would require taping for a year to make them stand. Not a hard job, the breeder assured us, easy to do. When we went down to South Jersey to pick her up, Grete pushed the other puppy aside in her rush to get out of the pen, bounded up to me, grabbed hold of my barn jacket, and pulled. Hard.

"She's pulling my jacket," I said to the breeder. "Ha, ha, ha."

"Just tell her no," said the breeder.

"No," I told Grete.

"Say it like you mean it," he said. "No!"

"No!" I said.

Grete smiled, I swear she did, and pulled harder.

Here was the next sign: Grete never napped. Aren't puppies supposed to nap? Aren't they supposed to run around and play really hard and then collapse in a heap of adorable warm puppy snoring that you can't resist hugging? Instead, Grete ran, and played, and leapt, and I was the one who got tired and laid down on the couch. Grete sat watching me. When I woke up an hour later, she was still staring at me.

Puppies are destructive. We knew that. But Grete was more than just destructive: She was clever and determined, and wasn't choosy. First she ripped off the Dixie cup taped to her ears to make them stand, like an arrogant prizefighter ripping off his robe before a bout. She set about chewing up shoes left on the floor, coasters off the coffee table, hardbacked books off the shelves. She tore a $20 bill into more than a dozen pieces. I tracked down all the bits and taped it back together like a jigsaw puzzle. Eric doubted the bank would take it. "They'll think we're drug dealers." Our

Grete

dog walker left a leather leash on top of Grete's crate. By the time we got home half the leash, including the handle, was gone. Grete discovered a garbage can containing used tampons, and we came home to a bedroom that looked like the scene of some unspeakable crime.

I met people who'd brag that they could put a steak on a countertop and their Great Danes would only drool. Not Grete. Because of her size, countertops were the perfect height for her to see food, grab food, and swallow food in less time than it takes to say, "No, no!" She ate anything and everything: Cheerios, potato chips, chicken breast, of course, but also yogurt, cucumber, salad with dressing. If you had it, she wanted it. She took food right off our plates. No, we said. No! We learned to eat defensively, at a raised countertop, our elbows cocked. We never left anything out. Toast for breakfast? Be sure to put the bread back in the drawer, the butter in the fridge, the knife in the dishwasher, and don't turn your back while executing any of these maneuvers. And never let your guard down.

Eric once made two turkey-and-swiss sandwiches for lunch and took them into the dining room. Heard a loud clanging in the kitchen. Got up to investigate and found Grete, paws in the sink, knife in her mouth. "No, Grete, no," he said, putting the knife in the dishwasher. By the time he got back to the dining room, both sandwiches were gone.

I read all the dog training books and talked to dog-owning friends. "Dogs hate loud sounds," one book said. "To deter undesired behavior, put coins in a can and shake it." We shook a can of coins and Grete looked at us blankly before lunging for the broccoli. "Squirt her mouth with vinegar." Grete just drooled. "Beat her," said my sister-in-law, the one with the docile fantasy Dane. I am ashamed to admit that I tried that, and it didn't work.

Like any conscientious, well-meaning pair of dog owners, we enrolled Grete and ourselves in puppy school at a local animal rescue facility and dog-handling school known for its skillful staff of professional trainers and therapists. She went through puppy kindergarten twice and two levels of advanced training. Grete proved able, even eager, to sit, lie down, heel, and stay as long as treats were involved. The instructor deemed her dominant-aggressive and told us Grete was determined to be alpha. The terminology sounded harsh to me. Sure, Grete was aggressive in her need to dominate. She demanded attention, pushing her face in ours. She was most comfortable on the couch and yielded her perch to no one. But she was never mean. She never snarled, or snapped, or showed her teeth. She was pesky and, because of her size, hugely so, but not scary.

"How bad can she really be?" asked my husband's mother. At a picnic by the pool at her house, we tried putting Grete in a fenced-in pen area, but she barked nonstop, and a Great Dane's bark is less than relaxing. "It's because she sees us," I said. So I took Grete around to the front of the house and secured her on her leash to a tree. Barking, yes, but a little less penetrating. Then silence, and our hopes lifted. Peace at last? Perhaps a minute passed. And then here she came, loping around the house, straight to the table, where my mother-in-law was making a point, gesticulating with a hot dog. "Watch your food," we said. "Watch your food!" Too late.

Why was our dog so bad? If it's true that you get the dog you deserve, what did having a domineering, willful, stubborn dog say about us? Doubts settled in. Was it because my husband let her sleep in our bed? Ask the dog books and they'll tell you absolutely, positively yes. And no. Was she some divine test of our patience? Or was she a 130-pound symbol that we were not really in control of our desires, our expectations, our destinies? Were we ourselves too mellow, allowing ourselves to be pushed around by a dog? Were we just passing through life, not taking charge? Or was I overthinking the torn-up wardrobe, the stolen Pop Tarts, the steamy dog breath beating in our faces whenever we sat on the toilet, judging ourselves and everything in our lives too acutely, if not too harshly? Maybe Grete was just a dog. A trying one, to be sure, but still. A dog.

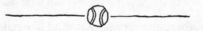

Life with an annoying dog had unexpected upsides, though. The dog whisperers at the training school said Grete had too much energy, which regular leash walks would not relieve. We needed to let her run, to exorcise her puppy demons. We started by putting her on a long clothesline (their suggestion) and taking her to a field, where she charged back and forth, frothing like a Tasmanian devil on methamphetamine. "Are you sure she's a Great Dane?" other dog people would ask. We used the clothesline until we made the happy discovery that a dominant-aggressive dog vying for leadership won't let her pack out of her sight. (We didn't find out, however, until after she charged a circle around me, trailing the clothesline. I had enough time to think, "Uh-oh," before the rope caught my ankle and jerked me off my feet. I landed on the ground, staring up at the sky.) We could walk her off leash, and she'd run up ahead but then come charging right back. On one nearby narrow trail, she'd race back and forth, and all we had to do was stand in place while she charged by.

The trail walks saved us. Walking a dog off leash in litigation-happy New Jersey is, of course, illegal just about everywhere. But even though we lived in the most densely populated state in the nation, I could take Grete to a wooded reservation and not see anyone at all. One of us took her on an hour-and-a-half hike every day, religiously, through every season. And like religion, it calmed and soothed our souls. Winter was the most peaceful, because with the leaves off the trees, I could see any oncoming hikers. Better yet, snow on the ground for footprints. Usually if we saw anyone at all, it was other walkers with dogs. I liked to think they too were allowing their dogs to work out all the frustrations of living in a confusing world where books were not meant to be torn from bindings and grilled cheese sandwiches were only for humans.

Another happy discovery of having an overconfident dog was her gentleness with children. Once, on a walk around the neighborhood, we came upon two young girls standing, as if waiting for us, in their driveway. One was about six, the other eight or ten, clearly with some developmental or mental disability, and overweight, bloated, likely from medications. They were eating popsicles and looked unafraid as Grete approached, a determined look in her eye. Their mother waved from the front porch. "It's okay," she said. "They're used to dogs. I'm a vet." The little girl with the disability held out her popsicle. Grete ate it with great tenderness. My heart swelled.

And as she aged, she did calm down. She was no longer in our faces every moment of every day. She started taking naps. She curled up on the couch after dinner. She still hovered whenever food was out, leaving stripes of slobber across the countertop, but she wasn't as fast on her feet, so you had a second to put the cream cheese back before she swiped your bagel.

Our hard-won peace was shattered, however, when we came home from China with an eleven-month-old girl. The baby threw all of Grete's most annoying tendencies into sharp relief. Grete couldn't understand why the baby had all the things that Grete wanted. Stuffed animals, for instance. Squeaky blocks. A paper-towel tube. Tupperware! Crackers, string cheese, slices of ham. Or why the baby was sleeping in Grete's bed. When the baby woke up in the middle of the night, Grete poked her with her nose, as if to say, "You're annoying me, go back to sleep." When the baby squealed with laughter, Grete rushed over and poked her butt, as if to say—what? I wasn't sure. Both baby and dog were obsessed with the dishwasher. While the baby hung on to the edge of its door, pushing and pulling the lower drawer in and out, in and out, Grete furiously licked the dishes. Frankly, they both annoyed me.

By the time you read this, Grete will likely no longer be ruling our lives. She is nine, old for a Dane. One week after we came home from China, we noticed she was limping. The doctors said she'd likely had a tumor in her tibia for a while. Stubborn Grete had refused to acknowledge anything was wrong. Right now, there's nothing to do for her except to manage her pain.

Dare I admit that I'll be slightly relieved? On the one hand, she is handsome, and I have the pride of peaceful walks with my dog by my side. But I will also be glad to be able to put noodles on the baby's tray without barricading her high chair. It can be frustrating when life refuses to play out the way you've fantasized it. Grete wasn't the Dane we'd envisioned. Our taxes are high. Our baby has come late in our lives. But you make adjustments as you walk along the path you've chosen. You learn to alter what it was you thought you wanted. And you hope the lessons you learn along the way come in handy at another time, in another way. Here's what Grete taught me: Don't leave a butter knife in the sink, and never turn your back.

Deadwood vs. Dogwood

Margaret Littman

I had been waiting for exactly seventy-two days for my heirloom striped Roman tomatoes to ripen. I bought the seedlings at the annual nonprofit organic plant sale at the Chicago Park District, and these weren't any old seedlings: The tiny plants cost twice what conventional tomatoes would at the local nursery.

But the cost was worth it. After all, this was the summer I was finally giving myself over to gardening. This was the year I invested in my backyard and went from just "having a garden" to actually referring to myself as a gardener. The year I described a new hard-to-find, tea-scented flower as the "Birkin bag of gardening." I could not be stopped. Neither, it soon became clear, could Natasha, my sixty-five-pound springer spaniel/ retriever mix.

On day forty-eight, the staked vines were loaded down with bright green oblong shapes striped with light yellow. According to the xeroxed chart the Park District gave to us, I knew that soon enough they would be sweet enough to eat like an apple or between bread in one of the Big Tomato Sandwiches in my favorite Deborah Madison cookbook.

Every couple days I'd make a tomato progress report as I walked through the garden to gather sun-ripened raspberries for breakfast. I also checked the progress of my peppers to see what color they had turned: green, red, yellow, or purple. Tiny yellow pear tomatoes dotted their vines like a string of tasteful Christmas lights. But I never saw a red striped Roman.

And then it was day seventy-five. My tomatoes were three days overdue. Natasha and I were taking an afternoon break in the backyard. We had played our daily game of soccer (the rules, I think, favor her, as she has four feet and no hands, and is more adept at moving things with her head). I was lying on the grass, looking up at the place where the magnolia tree branches tangle with the apple tree, becoming one giant figure eight–shaped tree from below.

Suddenly Natasha stood up, strolled over to the tomatoes, passed the yellow pears, and gingerly, without trampling or even bending the vine, picked a red-and-orange-striped Roman, hidden by some leaves, with her teeth. She leisurely carried it across the yard to a shady spot, placed it between her front paws, and began to eat. No basil or mozzarella necessary.

She seemed to savor it, eating more slowly than she (or any dog) usually does when having an off-limits snack. I started to shout the "drop it" command, but I didn't want a half-eaten tomato, and I figured that someone should get to enjoy the fruits of my labor.

Even as I realized that she had enjoyed all those other (ripe or not) striped Romans that had seemed so promising fifteen days earlier (confirmation came weeks later, when seeds from the tomatoes started to sprout in Natasha's favorite place to relieve herself), I still couldn't get mad at her. I'm patient when she tramples the bee balm, pees on the hydrangea, and eats the striped Romans, forsaking all other produce, because without her I wouldn't have a garden. Without her I wouldn't be a gardener.

I bought the tiny 1950s brick Georgian with a larger-than-standard yard because I wanted a place where Natasha and Boris, a sixty-pound collie mix who has since passed, could run. A yard was merely a place to let the dogs out so that you didn't have to take late-night walks dressed in a pea coat over a nightgown or in below-freezing temperatures. Yards were a place you kept the grill. But that was before I was responsible for a yard; I realized rather quickly that the meticulously straight rows of tulips and phlox planted by the previous owners were not going to survive a single game of fetch, much less a season. After just one spring of tying the spent green daffodil stems into neat, asparagus-like bunches so the stalks would fertilize the bulbs before they went dormant, I began to contemplate the allure of trample-proof AstroTurf.

Natasha

I came by this gardening ignorance naturally. The weekend I moved in, my parents came to visit. In an effort to help out, my mother pulled out my hand-me-down push mower and cut the grass. She was fifty-eight years old, and this was the first time she had ever mowed a lawn. Clearly, I did not inherit a love of gardening passed down through generations.

Instead, it was Natasha who showed me how to embrace my inner gardener. I quickly figured out that planting identical foliage in straight rows was for pet-free homeowners. This design calls attention to the sad plant that has been peed on or dug up . . . or dug up and then peed on. Having curves and organic shapes in garden design makes such flaws less noticeable. It's the horticultural equivalent of having curly hair; no one notices if your bangs aren't quite even. Like my perennially messy hair, the organic shape started to look like I knew what I was doing. By not trying to force grass to grow where it didn't want to grow, such as under a tree where Natasha naps every day, I transformed a worn, shady patch into a shade-loving woodland bed. Underneath the magnolia tree, hosta leaves grow as big as my head, ferns reach as tall as my waist, and vinca doesn't mind being a pillow between a spaniel and the ground on a hot day.

My transformation from someone who owns a garden to a gardener was official when I opted to buy new Proven Winner perennials for summer instead of new Cole Haan sandals. Suddenly, I began to collect the clumps of white and black dog fur on my couch for the compost pile instead of brushing it away (finally, a real use for that shed fur!).

Five years later, I'm contemplating becoming certified as a master gardener. I have made applesauce for a sick neighbor with apples from my tree, and I have supplied fresh mint three years in a row for an annual Kentucky Derby party (mint juleps for everyone!). I have woken at 7:00 AM on a Saturday to drive across town for a great deal on a new compost bin. When an out-of-town friend came to visit and initially drove past my house, not recognizing the drastic changes I had made to the landscape, the compliment was much better than if he had said, "You look great! Have you lost weight?"

While Natasha has brought me closer to the garden, the garden has helped me understand her better. When friends began commenting regularly on how green my grass is, despite the fact that I don't have a dog run and let Natasha pee wherever she wants, I took credit. I thought this was a sign of my fabulous gardening skills, my regular aeration, mulching, and refusal to overwater. In fact, the grass wasn't turning yellow because she had a kidney infection that caused her urine to be diluted. When she couldn't stop munching the striped spider grass, it wasn't because I had cultivated some new sweet variety; it was only that she was trying to calm an upset stomach.

I learned that while Natasha is afraid of horses (we stay away from mounted police) and fiberglass animals (we also avoid mini putt-putt courses), she is fearless when chasing away raccoons, possums, and feral cats. Even the scent of fox and coyote urine, bought on eBay to keep the critters away, fails to give her pause.

I learned that all the training classes and commands in the world cannot stop a dog with retriever genes from interrupting a game of croquet.

I learned that if she leaves a rawhide outside at 11:00 PM, there is a 92 percent chance that she'll wake up and remember it at 3:15 AM and will need to go retrieve it before someone else does.

And unlike me, who mourns the months of December

through March because they mean I can't dig, prune, shape, or create, Natasha is as drawn to the garden in winter as she is in summer. If she wakes up in the middle of the night to see fresh snow falling, she'll immediately want to run out to make snow dog-angels.

Not since I worked holed up in a darkroom in college have I had a hobby that has enabled me to ignore my watch and forget how much time has passed. I found something I loved more than writing, more than reading, more than almost anything else (except Natasha, of course). The garden is something I want to talk about, to the point of joining listservs to trade tips, discuss the best source for live beneficial insects, and learn bad gardening jokes. (What's a perennial? An annual that doesn't die.)

I'm still searching, though, for a recipe that calls for both barren tomato stems and dog hair.

My Dog,
My Divorce Doctor

Tricia O'Brien

I can recall plenty of days over that fall and winter that I did not want to get out of bed. Instead, I dreamed of hiding out, seeking permanent refuge under the safety of my covers.

But as I lay there, I would feel that furry pile of warmth at the foot of my bed, and I'd hear *thwomp, thwomp* as her tail flapped on the comforter. And with that, I was able to muster a smile, make my way to the coffeemaker, and prepare myself to face the outside world.

It was 2003, and I was living with my then-two-year-old golden retriever, Lyle, at my parents' shore house; they had returned to Texas for the colder months. Although it was only sixty-five miles from Manhattan, the seaside town seemed sleepy, windswept, and far away without the throngs of bicycle-riding, bathing suit–clad summer residents. This solitary place, almost like my own island of exile, was just what I needed at the time. And besides, I wasn't alone: I had Lyle.

After three years in Seattle, my ex-husband and I had relocated to Washington, D.C. Although we loved it out West, I missed my family and friends back East, and he had found a great career opportunity in D.C. Our one-year-old marriage was fragile, to say the least, and I hoped that a change of scenery might give us a shot at a second chance. Those two weeks in D.C. told me otherwise. At the end of my rope, I loaded Lyle into the car along with some clothing and photos, and we made the four-hour drive to the shore. I didn't know how long I would be there or what my next move might be—all I knew was that I needed some time to decompress. Although I eventually returned to New York City, where I lived before moving to Seattle, I wasn't ready to make that decision right away.

Each morning, I bundled up in fleece, Gore-Tex, and a hat and we walked across the street to the beach—or rather, she pulled me toward the Atlantic, guided by her puppy compass, huffing and puffing with excitement. She would plow ahead, pulling the leash taut, and then look back at me, as if checking on me.

Once we hit the beach, I'd unclip her leash, and she would

pounce, front paws low, butt in the air, beckoning me to *throw the ball already* in her loud-and-clear puppy language. She'd let out a shrill bark, tail wagging furiously behind her, her face lit up like a child's on Christmas. She'd run recklessly, happily, with abandon after the tennis ball. It was at these moments, as I watched Lyle each morning on the beach, that I was able to tap into what seemed to be eluding me, what was buried somewhere deep inside me: For the time being, watching Lyle experience joy was as close to the emotion as I could get, and even taking baby steps toward it felt good.

I'd never known depression, really. But the meltdown of my marriage, the shattering of my dreams for the future, and all the failure that seemed wrapped up in my impending divorce had sent me into a downward spiral. Sure, I'd experienced loss before: I'd been brokenhearted over breakups or disappointed upon being passed over for a promotion. I'd received a pink slip after an employer went belly-up, and I'd seen all four of my grandparents laid in the ground. But this feeling that had set in after my separation was different. It was like a heavy fog that wouldn't lift. And as much as I tried to rationalize it away, or journal it away, or talk it away with a therapist, there it stayed.

My feelings could change depending on the day, or even the moment. Sometimes a giant wave of anger overtook me, and I wanted to scream at the top of my lungs that I hated him. Other days, many times, I felt hurt that this person I had loved, and had taken vows to spend the rest of my life with, had disappointed me so supremely. Still other times, I was just utterly confused: *Who was I now?* This whole life that I thought was charted for me had completely changed course. I was single again. I needed

Lyle

to figure out where to live. And I was contemplating leaving behind the flexibility of freelance writing to return to the more stable (and less isolating) life of a magazine editor. But even amid these feelings of despair, confusion, and anger, I was lucid about one thing: The decision to leave my marriage had been a painstaking one, something I had put much thought into. And it felt right, regardless of how difficult this time was for me.

During those cold months, one thing, one being, could always lift me, even if temporarily, out of the funk. Lyle had basic needs: food, exercise, and love. And she needed me. I could provide all of this. And while she wanted to make me happy, I didn't have to put on a happy face for her. She let me just *be*.

My family and friends wanted me to be happy too. They

said, "You should be relieved you two didn't have kids together. That would be even more complicated." (True, but what if I never experience motherhood—beyond the canine variety, that is?) Or, "You're lucky to have the support network you do." (True again, but being the first of my peers to go through a divorce, I felt alone.) Or, "You just have to put it behind you and move on."

Put it. Behind. You. And move. On. The very idea was daunting. There were so many disappointments tied up in the end of my marriage. I thought, *Will I ever have another shot at marriage and a family?* I felt like I didn't fit in in many ways, because many of my friends (not to mention two of my sisters) were married with families.

During this time, Lyle was the main constant in my life. When I went out, she'd be waiting for me in the window when I returned home. Shaking her backside, her tail wagged back and forth; she couldn't wait to see me. She looked up at me with those gorgeous brown eyes, rimmed by long, blondish-red eyelashes and what looks like kohl. When I wrote at my desk, she'd lie outstretched on the floor next to me. And at those times when I spontaneously burst into tears, she hurried to my side, and looked at me as if to say, *What can I do?*

But that was just it. Her being there, her knowing me, her needing me, was what I needed. On those many days when I didn't want to get out of bed, I knew she needed me to take her for a walk. I knew she would be happy to swim in the ocean and romp on the beach. And I knew that once we got to the beach, I would be thankful to Lyle.

Even on days when fierce winds sprayed the sand and I fought to walk against their force, I'd look out at the Atlantic and feel a sense of calm wash over me. I was able to build hope. To find strength. To feel trickles of emotion inside of me that somehow seemed dead. And though these feelings might be short-lived, gone when we left the beach, I was able to gather some hope that I could feel again.

As the temperatures dropped, we still continued to make daily excursions to the beach. Each day Lyle chased the tennis ball and the gulls, swam in the water (which turned to icicles on her fur on the coldest of days), and sprayed sand behind her as she dug, looking for what seemed like buried puppy treasure. I walked with her on the sand, my footsteps leaving behind an impression. It somehow gave me solace: At a time when I felt inconsequential, like how could I be real, how could my life be real, I could see I really was there. And I had left behind footsteps to prove it.

In January, I started training for a marathon, with Lyle as my partner on five- to six-mile jaunts by the water's edge. For every mile I covered, she probably racked up five. She bounded into the water, where she would swim out to a pack of seagulls. As she got near them, they would flap away. She'd paddle off in another direction, thinking she could find other birds to play with. And then she would come back to the sand, run alongside me, until a bird intersected our course and off she went, legs in perfect motion like I occasionally felt when I was running at a good clip, kicking up sand in her wake. I could feel a smile stretch across my face.

After her beach sessions, she usually had a two-minute burst of lingering energy that she would burn off by running out on the back deck in figure eights, gathering lightning speed. And then she crashed, into a heap of fur on the floor—either in her favorite corner, or maybe on the bed, both of which were within eyeshot of my desk. I'd glance over at her, and without getting up, she would look back, and *thwomp, thwomp* her tail. It was her way of telling me, *Everything is going to be okay.*

Sixth Sense?

Gail Hulnick

I collapse on the bed, exhausted from another day of chasing a preschooler and a toddler. My day started at 5:30 AM and now, at 8:00 PM, it's almost history. It's a very busy phase in our lives—and soon, I discover, it will get even busier.

Casey, my five-year-old keeshond, arrives at the side of the bed and puts his nose into my hand. He waits for an invitation, then leaps up on the foot of the bed. Walking carefully—almost as if on tiptoe, if there is such a thing for dogs—he moves toward my head. I turn onto my left side, he steps over me, and settles his middle against mine.

Casey was our first step toward family life. Before our children arrived, he was the one who gave us a glimpse into what parenthood required. Once he took possession of his spot in our kitchen, I started adding quite a bit to the five minutes a day that I usually spent there. Before he landed in our lives, almost all food and drink were picked up on the run. Lunches from the office cafeteria, dinners at a local restaurant or café. My husband and I were on different work schedules, with my day as a radio broadcaster starting before dawn and his as a lawyer often lasting late into the evening. We worked hard, belonged to clubs, went to a lot of meetings and social events. Home was where the clothes were.

Babies change all that—and so do dogs.

We brought Casey home when he was eight weeks old and I was more than ready to cut back on the number of hours we spent in public places. We both started to eat dinner at home every night and to shape our schedules around his needs. Morning, noon, early-afternoon, and late-night walks punctuated the day. We scheduled shopping trips to keep him supplied with food, equipment, and toys; visits to the doggy doctor; and special afternoons at the dog park. At the time, he seemed like a good test of my readiness to settle down. A practice baby, if you will.

One night when Casey was about three months old, he vaulted up onto our bed, where I was stretched out, propped up on one elbow. Instead of his usual routine of turning around three times and landing with a happy sigh and a *thump* at the foot of the bed, he just stood there, looking at me.

"What's wrong with you?" I talked to him all the time, as most pet owners do, I imagine. (After all, you rarely get a cranky reply or attitude from a dog.) "Come on, lie down, Casey."

He stood for a good two minutes before complying. But when he did, he didn't choose his usual spot. He put his front paws in front of me, his back paws behind me, and sank down across my middle.

While the position was unusual, it turned out to be very comfortable. And it became his favorite spot in the evenings, before the lights went out and he jumped down to the floor. Every night for the next two weeks, there he was, like a soft, warm blanket. Keeshonds are a double-coated breed with beautiful black, gray, and cream markings, particularly around the eyes, where the black lines look like spectacles. They are also one of the "smiling" breeds, and when he cuddled up on me, stared into my eyes, and panted away, pulling his lips back over his teeth, it looked as though he was beaming his approval.

Did he know before we did? When the doctor told me that I was pregnant shortly thereafter, the question didn't even cross my mind. I had enough to think about, with morning sickness making unexpected appearances and waves of fatigue rising to submerge me every day from about noon on. Plus, there were baby clothes to buy, cribs and change tables to check out, names to consider.

And every night, Casey came to straddle my waist in his new favorite spot. The months passed, my belly expanded, and he had to stretch a little farther to take up his position. Then, when I was around five months along, he stopped jumping up on the bed. It

Casey

seemed to be right around the time that I first felt the kicking and rolling inside, but I couldn't be sure. Maybe he thought I'd just become too big for him to stretch over. For whatever reason, that seemed to be the end of things for my pregnancy pal. He still liked to curl up on my feet when I sat in a chair, and to crawl into my lap (what was left of it) during a thunderstorm. But no more bedtime "hugs."

Once the baby came, Casey was my shadow as I went about my day's routine. Even in the middle of the night, for a feeding that happened only an hour after the previous one, he was there. He liked his sleep, no question, but he woke up instantly whenever the baby cried.

It took us about six months to get used to this new being in the house. But gradually, eventually, we were back into a familiar rhythm. Then one evening Casey suddenly appeared, standing on the bed again, staring at my face as if it had suddenly turned blue. He stepped cautiously over me and lowered his weight, now that he was nearly three years old, up to about fifty pounds. And yes, I was pregnant with child number two.

For the next four months, he was once again my bun-in-the-oven buddy. We all find an item (or two or three) to help ease the challenges of pregnancy: comfort foods, soothing music, distracting movies, books, or places. And yes, I ate my share of pickles, ice cream, and chocolate. But at times, nothing worked. Not looking at photos of other people's cute babies, not cuddling with my own, not listening to Vivaldi while soaking in a warm, vanilla-scented bath. When I was so tired or nauseated that none of the usual comforts worked, I could always count on Casey.

At about the same point as in the first pregnancy, when the baby started moving inside, Casey's regular tummy-straddling visits ended. He still dogged my footsteps as I ran around the house, chasing my two-year-old and feeding the laundry monster, but no more bedtimes with the "bump."

Until this evening, early in the winter. He follows me upstairs at bath time and stands outside the door, staring, until I close it on him so that I can focus on the kiddies in the tub. When I open it half an hour later, he hasn't moved. When I go into the bedroom to lie down, he jumps up, as if on springs, and settles down on me. Instant doggy blanket.

And was he right? Yep. Canine pregnancy test—three for three. And during that third time around, he looked after me just as devotedly as during the first two, with one difference: Even after the baby started moving, he continued to give me his version of a hug. Did he guess that this would be the last time, and had he decided not to give up his job as prenatal comforter until he absolutely had to? Or did he have some sense that this one, headed for a difficult delivery, needed more cuddling and doggy hugs than most? He kept it up until I was so huge that his little paws barely touched the bed on either side of me.

Casey lived for another eleven years, and although he jumped up on the bed many more times, he never again played doggy blanket.

How to
Banish Melancholy

Abigail Thomas

You will need three dogs, one of whom has caught the scent of something interesting wafting through the second floor window. She is a hound. They are all hounds, and the four of you sleep together on a double bed. When you open your eyes (her warm doggy breath on your face), she will be staring at you with such intensity that you burst out laughing. You will throw on yesterday's clothes (which are lying conveniently on the floor) and head downstairs without tripping over Rosie, Harry, or Carolina, all of whom are underfoot. When you open the kitchen door they will fly into the yard and immediately commence hunting, noses to the ground, some small creature whose zigzagging trail resembles an electrocardiogram. You follow them onto the wet green lawn. So now you're outdoors and it's 5:00 AM.

For the last month you've been inside while it rained. Perhaps you are a fan of rain, but this may have gone on too long. You have stopped answering your phone. You don't gather the mail. You have noticed that bad as it was when two dogs followed you from room to room, it's even worse with three. You got the third dog two weeks ago, a hound found living at a rest stop in South Carolina. Every time you get up, they get up. Please don't, it's not worth it, you want to say as you rise from your soft red chair to wander into the kitchen on an errand you forget before arriving. You look out the window while the dogs settle down in a sunny spot by the stove. They are so good-natured. Moments later you head back to the soft red chair, perhaps holding a glass of water or perhaps not, and again the dogs trail along behind, and if you do this often enough, the aimlessness of your day is driven home. From here it is but a hop, skip, and a jump to the pointlessness of your existence, which is why it is so excellent to be outdoors with your clothes on at five this morning.

Next you will need a bed of nettles five feet high. Perhaps you already have a garden like this, having neglected it for the two years you have lived in the country. You have told yourself that you don't want to put anything into the ground so you will not have to hate the deer who will certainly eat it, but the fact is, you are bone lazy and prefer drinking coffee and sitting on the stoop to weeding or raking or digging a hole. But nettles have closed over the heads of three pink peony bushes you could swear you saw two summers ago, and you are experiencing an unfamiliar surge of energy. You dash inside (the dogs still poking around with tails high, and you realize in passing you love even their assholes) and good, there they are, the gardening gloves given to you as a housewarming present two years ago, still stapled together. You rip them apart, don them, and charge back into the yard.

Harry

Your first nettle comes up with the perfect amount of resistance: none. You can yank it out by the roots and you do so, flinging it with joy behind you. You yank another and another and pretty soon you are a madwoman, pulling nettles three at a time, caring nothing for the stinging on your arms and ankles, and the mound grows on the grass behind you. Sometimes you get a stubborn old grandfather and, pulling as hard as you can, you reach the big root snaking just under the surface and get that too, dirt flying as you tear it out, and now you are *the old woman and the nettle*, destroyer and giver of life, you are *once upon a time there lived*, and you understand the ferocity of the gardener.

After five or six minutes you will tire and stand back from your work. A tiny patch has been thinned. Perhaps you will now make coffee and bring the cup outside. If all goes well, a perfect pink peony bush will be revealed by lunchtime. There will be slim yellow irises too, and the big throaty purple ones that remind you, alas, of an old man's scrotum, but you will weed there too. By early afternoon the sun may burn through what has been a heavy mist, and should you not be ready to be dazzled, do not fret. It's time for a nap anyway. Inside you may notice that what you thought was dust is instead a layer of golden pollen blowing through the open windows. *If only life were more like this,* you will think, as you and the dogs traipse up to bed, and then you realize with a start that this is life.

The Truth About Cops and Dogs

Rebecca Skloot

Eight months ago, if you'd told me I'd be obsessed with a little old Greek guy and fantasizing about killing his dogs, I'd have said you were nuts. If you'd said a little old Greek guy's pack of eight junkyard dogs had been roaming the streets of midtown Manhattan for years, attacking people and tearing apart their dogs while city officials said, "Sorry, that's not *our* problem," I'd have called you a conspiracy theorist. A pack of wild dogs? In Manhattan? Never happens. Boy, would I have been wrong.

Here's how I know: The Sunday before Christmas, I woke up to my friend Elizabeth pounding frantically on my door. She was staying at my apartment—that morning, as I'd slept, she'd taken my dog, Bonny, for a walk. When I opened the door, Elizabeth stood clutching Bonny's empty, bloody collar and screaming, "Something awful happened!" I bolted into the hallway wearing nothing but underwear, heading toward the snow and ice to find my dog. Elizabeth grabbed my shoulder: "It's cold out." I spun around, grabbed a blanket, cell phone, and credit card, threw a long down coat over my underwear, then ran barefoot out the door.

My doorman looked to the ground, whispering, "I'm sorry" over and over; Ralphie, my maintenance man, pointed toward a small courtyard behind the building. "A pack of dogs," he whispered as I ran past. "Huge dogs." That's when I saw the first puddle of blood and the fist-size chunk of Bonny's muscle on the sidewalk. "They eat her," Ralphie yelled after me. "Don't look."

I was a veterinary technician for ten years. I started off vaccinating and x-raying people's pets but eventually left general practice for a vet school, where I worked in the morgue performing daily autopsies, then became an adrenaline-pumped emergency room tech who did CPR on dying dogs and used words like "code red" and "stat." I'd seen animals bigger than Bonny literally torn in half by packs; I'd seen missing limbs and decapitations; I'd done autopsies on dogs who'd eaten children and documented the contents of their stomachs for police reports. Which is all to say, when I heard the phrase "pack of dogs," I had clear visuals of what I was about to find.

I ran into the courtyard, yelling Bonny's name, trying not to look at the blood-smeared walkway. I heard her crying before I saw her, quivering in a pool of blood behind a small bush, eyes wide, intestines hanging through a hole in her side. She screamed as I scooped her up, wrapped her in the blanket and lowered her onto a picnic table. That's when the vet tech in me took over. I didn't feel emotions or my bare feet in the snow. I just lifted the blanket, checked her heart rate, pupils, and the color of her gums. I thought clinical terms like *lacerations, puncture wounds,* and *decreased capillary refill time,* but the reality was, they'd bitten her so many times it looked like she'd been sprayed with machine-gun fire. They crushed her pelvis and ripped her body open from hip to armpit on both sides. They slit her throat so deep I could see her jugular vein. They sank their teeth into each of her thighs and pulled her legs in opposite directions, detaching her muscles from her bones. They ripped and tore until Ralphie heard the screams, grabbed a two-by-four, and ran outside swinging. When he got there, Bonny had the biggest dog by the throat, but its jaws were twice the size of hers, and wrapped around her neck. The others were going for Bonny's intestines. No mistake: They were going to eat her.

A few months before my seventeenth birthday, my best friend and I went to a grocery store for some coffee and eggs and came home with Bonny instead. We adopted her in the parking lot, straight from a cardboard box in the trunk of a rusted-out Chevy with a sign that said FREE PUPS. Her littermates squealed and climbed over each other, but Bonny just stared at us, eyes locked,

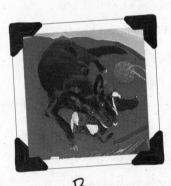

Bonny

knowing full well she was supposed to go home with us, just waiting for us to figure it out. She was maybe three pounds, with ears so huge and pointy they met in the middle of her head, like one giant ear. We named her after the remote hill outside Portland, Oregon, where we lived—Bonny Slope. With time, as her ears continued to grow, we'd call her "Radar," "Satellite Dish," or "Bat Dog," and she'd answer to each one.

Now, Bonny looks like a jackal, with a lean body built for running through endless nights. She's a thirty-five-pound lap dog who refuses to go out in the rain and tiptoes around mud puddles, but loves full-contact wrestling, scaling trees after squirrels, and running commando through the woods. She's lithe and graceful as a greyhound, even at fifteen. She was all black until about seven years ago, when her muzzle started to gray, then her chest, then feet. She's part border collie—a dog bred for keeping its herd safe, riding on the backs of sheep and weaving between the hooves of stampeding cattle, nipping heels to keep everyone running straight.

Border collies are known for having eyes so intense, they can lock onto a stray bull and maneuver it back into a herd. Bonny's got that stare. She's turned it on me many times: When my house caught on fire, when a man tried jimmying the lock of my hotel room. She uses it at least once a week when we walk the streets, locking those chestnut eyes on mine, like *Don't ask questions, just follow,* then pressing her body against me, putting herself between me and whatever she doesn't like, and steering me home, sometimes using streets she's never walked.

Bonny is a worrier: eyebrows always wrinkled, ears in constant motion—one second they're flat against her head, like *I'm sorry!* then straight up, like *Oh my God!* Then one flat and the other rotated 180 degrees, like *Oh no, what's going on back there?* And I'm her biggest worry: In the last year we'd moved from one city to the next; we'd gone from three-bedroom house to tiny apartment, divorced my husband, and cried together as my other fifteen-year-old dog, Sereno, died in my arms. Which is to say, I'd become Bonny's entire herd, and she'd become mine.

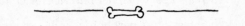

Minutes after the attack, I held Bonny in the back seat of Elizabeth's car and screamed at her to ignore the one-way signs and red lights. After crawling through forty-six blocks of gridlocked Christmas-week traffic to the only hospital open on Sundays, and after Bonny went into the surgery doctors said she probably wouldn't wake up from, I did two things. I looked down at my blood-covered self, still barefoot and naked except for a coat, and I actually laughed. It was a deep, disturbed, this-isn't-really-happening kind of laugh. Then I lost it.

The next thing I remember is Elizabeth saying we should call the police, and me thinking, *Damn right*. She called 911.

"Sorry," the dispatcher told her, "We don't handle dog-on-dog complaints. We can't do anything unless they bite a person. Call Animal Control."

So she did. "Dog-on-dog attacks aren't our jurisdiction," they told her. "Call the ASPCA."

So she did. "We don't handle dog-versus-dog attacks," they said. "Call Animal Control."

Elizabeth laughed. "They just told me to call you."

"Okay, then call your police precinct."

Elizabeth got the tenth precinct on the phone and said

she'd like to file a complaint. "Sorry," he told her, "we only take human complaints, you can't file a complaint for a dog. Call the Department of Health." So she did, and guess what they said: "We don't handle dog-on-dog complaints. You should call 911."

Elizabeth sat down next to me and stared at her phone like it'd just done the craziest thing. "What'd they say?" I asked. "They said you should call back on Monday," she told me after a long pause. "The weekend people are clueless."

That night, with Bonny still unconscious after hours of touch-and-go surgery, I walked into the lobby of my apartment and overheard two neighbors talking. See the blood on the sidewalk? they said. Harry's pack did it again. This time they killed some dog named Bonny. Ate her alive.

I stopped. "Excuse me," I said, "did you say *Harry's* dogs?"

"Yeah," one woman said, shaking her head, "That homeless asshole's crazy pack of dogs has attacked a bunch of people and mauled, what, a dozen dogs?"

The other neighbor nodded. "At least."

"They've been attacking people for years," my doorman said. "You know Andrew up in 14B? They got him last month, bit all over his arms and legs, sent him to the hospital. The city won't do anything about it."

I asked if anyone had called the police and they laughed, like

Silly girl. The woman, who insisted I not use her name, whispered, "You want my advice? Throw rat poison into the lot. That's the only way you're gonna get results. While you're at it, throw some poison in for Harry. It's his fault they're like this."

Harry Theodore was born Theocharas Paleologos on a Macedonian goat farm and raised in Greece, where he trained Doberman pinschers to hunt and kill wild boar. He came to America at eighteen with dreams of becoming an engineer, then went from factory job to longshoreman to hot dog vendor. Business never did take off because his cart was always surrounded by a pack of German shorthaired pointers. Harry started breeding them in the '60s, when a friend gave him two dogs that he bred and inbred until, at one point, he had more than fifty.

Harry's in his late sixties now, five feet five inches tall, with a leathery face covered in gray stubble. He and his dogs live on 36th Street just east of 11th Avenue, a few blocks from my apartment, in a junkyard full of rusted hot dog carts and car parts, scraps of rotting linoleum, mildewed blankets, rats, and piles of garbage he scrounges from neighborhood markets to feed his dogs. The lot was part of a shanty town until the city cleared it in 1997; Harry moved in later that year, when he got kicked out of an abandoned house on the East Side. He used to sleep in a plywood shack in the back of the lot, but it burned down a few years ago. After that, neighbors say, he started sleeping in a gutted van. They also say Harry subsidizes his social security checks by selling puppies, but that he doesn't sell to police officers—they get dogs for free.

I've never talked to Harry—I kept myself anonymous so I could sit across the street from his lot on a loading dock, watching him and his dogs. Which is what I did the night Bonny was attacked, right after my neighbors told me where he lived. I expected I'd want to kill Harry's dogs when I finally saw them, but I didn't. I wanted to hurt Harry. His dogs were covered in sores and scars; one had a huge tumor on its lip, others had what looked like a broken leg, a dislocated or malformed jaw, and hugely swollen joints—maybe from arthritis, maybe just from generations of inbreeding. Their coats were dingy and thin, like they'd been malnourished and riddled with mange or mites for years. Two males fought over a piece of bread crust. A female cowered as I walked up to the gate, then scooted away, barely lifting her hips from the ground because her arthritis hurt too bad to stand.

I went home, typed "Harry Theodore" into a few search engines, and couldn't believe what I found: a feature-length profile *The New York Times* ran in 1994, and a small news story in the

New York Daily News. These were not stories about a man with a dangerous pack of dogs; they were about Harry, a colorful and quintessentially New York character, a poor homeless man who could barely feed himself, yet opened his heart to the countless dogs he kept happy, healthy, and walking leashless throughout the city, like a "shepherd . . . watching his flock." Through these articles and endless talks with neighbors, I slowly learned Harry's story.

He says he's sixty-nine years old, and from his clouded eyes to his slow, tortured, arthritic walk, I believe it. But my neighbors don't. They believe Harry's age as much as they buy the heart condition, asthma, and ulcers he uses to explain why he can't leash or kennel his dogs—his body and wallet can't handle it, he says. "That's insulting," my neighbor yelled, "But you know what really gets me? I'm payin' sky-high rent and I've gotta worry about being mauled by a homeless guy's pack of dogs? Gimme a break! With all the rent and taxes I pay, you'd think I'd be able to call the city and say, 'This homeless guy's dogs are terrorizing us,' and that they'd do something about it." But no one does.

The morning after the attack, I sat down with my phone and notebook and started what would become months' worth of calls to the same string of organizations: the NYPD, the Department of Health, Animal Control, ASPCA and the mayor's office. The Department of Health knew all about Harry's dogs—they'd recently taken a report of his dogs' biting a man. I told the story to Officer Baldino at the NYPD's tenth precinct, and he said, "Oh, yeah, I know who you're talking about. Those dogs are really bad—I don't know why they don't stop them."

"Who's *they*?" I asked. "Aren't you *they*?"

"No, you call . . . wait a minute, I don't know who you call." Then he lowered the phone. "Hey, guys, you know that dog pack on 36th? Lady here's tryin' to figure out who to call about getting rid of them. ASPCA? She did that; you know what they said? They said they don't do dog-on-dog. They say we do." Then he turned back to me and said, "Call the ASPCA again. I'm surprised they're not helping you." So I talked to Giselle at the ASPCA's animal law division—the organization featured on Animal Planet's *Animal Precinct*. "Oh, right," she said, "we get complaints about him all the time." Turns out an ASPCA officer was at the lot in response to another complaint just days before Bonny was attacked. He found no evidence of a problem. "It's embarrassing," one ASPCA operator told me, "but the city has no law against dogs mutilating other dogs."

I simply didn't believe that. So I decided to turn myself into an authority on dog law: I studied the history of dog law and how it differs from state to state. Dangerous dogs (i.e., dogs that should be contained or confiscated) are defined in the New York City administrative code as "any dog with a known propensity, tendency, or disposition to attack when unprovoked, to cause injury, or to otherwise endanger the safety of human beings or domestic animals." Sounds straightforward. But the problem is, not all relevant city and state laws list biting domestic animals as an offense. Even if they did, dogs don't qualify as domestic animals in New York—they're considered property. The inconsistent laws and that definition of domestic animal—a holdover many states did away with years ago—in effect create a loophole city organizations can point to and say, *See, there's no law against dog-on-dog attacks*. The truth is, the city could tackle dog-on-dog crime under any number of laws. But it doesn't.

I talked to animal law experts from all over the country, like David Favre, a law professor at Michigan State University who runs the Animal Legal and Historical Center. "I'm shocked that New York animal law is as backwards as it is," he told me. "New York is usually pretty progressive." But, he said, regardless of that loophole, "If the city wanted to do something, it could. The dogs are clearly a nuisance—they've bitten people, and even if they hadn't, New York law says any police or peace officer shall seize any dog that poses a threat to public safety. And these dogs do."

When I explained the situation to Marie Mar, an attorney with the Bar Association's Committee on Legal Issues Pertaining to Animals, she said, "What you're dealing with is selective law enforcement—the only reason you're not getting action is that nobody wants to deal with it." Then she rattled off some of the many reasons Harry's dogs should be confiscated: leash laws, public nuisance, destruction of private property, imminent threat to humans. "They'll come get these dogs in a second when they kill a person, but it shouldn't have to get that far."

Kenneth Phillips, an attorney and author of the books *Dog Bite Law* and *What to Do If Your Dog Is Injured or Killed,* nearly threw the phone in disgust when he heard about Harry's dogs. "Canine behaviorists have shown time and time again that dog packs hone their hunting skills in a series of escalating attacks that start with other animals, then often turn to humans, which means this could easily result in a dead adult or child, and probably will."

———————— ✗ ————————

My neighbor Andrew Lauffer was attacked only a month before Bonny. "There were so many of them I couldn't see the ground around me," he told me. "They were all biting me, biting my dogs." Harry's pack cornered Bob Lee on an icy sidewalk and ripped pieces out of his dog's flank. And they surrounded sixty-seven-year-old Richard Foster on his stoop: "Fourteen of them came out of nowhere," he told me. "They knocked me over and pinned me down so I couldn't move." Then they went after his dog, tearing several holes in its side.

Five years ago, in response to the attacks, Bob, Richard, and at least ten other neighbors formed a group called The Neighbors Concerned with the Dog Pack Attacks. They spent two and a half years fighting to get Harry's dogs taken away. They complained to the city and testified at community-board hearings in front of the Department of Health (and Harry)—one man even testified that he'd seen Harry beat his dogs with large metal poles. The community board asked Harry to keep his dogs confined. And that was it. Harry didn't comply, no one made him, and eventually The Neighbors gave up.

One morning after Bonny came home from the hospital—after eighty-seven stitches, more than a week in intensive care, and $7,000 in vet bills—my doorman called and said, "Don't come downstairs, Rebecca. Harry's dogs are pacing out front." I grabbed my cell phone and a carving knife, in case they came after me, then ran downstairs. But they were gone. I called Animal Control.

"Where are the dogs now?" the dispatcher asked.

"I don't know, but they can't be far," I said. "They're probably headed for the lot."

"Sorry," he said, "we can't come pick up the dogs unless they're loose and you know where they are." And I snapped: Bonny was covered neck to tail in bandages and bruises. She couldn't walk, and no one knew if she ever would. And my neighbors were afraid to let their children outside. But no one would do a damn thing about the dogs.

That's when I ran back to my apartment and did something most people can't do. I called press offices, saying, "Hi, I'm a reporter writing an article about a pack of dangerous dogs that's been roaming the streets attacking people and dogs for years. Numerous people have filed complaints with your organization, and I'd like to find out why nothing has been done." Suddenly, they actually started paying attention. But mainly, they made excuses: budget problems, not our jurisdiction, not enough officers. "It's like, forget about it," the head of Animal Control told me. "I've only got one officer covering all of Manhattan and The Bronx. Unless we're right in the area, it's impossible to get there in time." Dangerous dog law enforcement and funds allocation is the Department of Health's jurisdiction, he told me (and he was right). "If these dogs maul someone tomorrow, it's going to be like, 'Hey, you warned everybody, you told them what was happening.' If that happens

because there weren't enough bodies to take care of the problem
... well ... " Then he paused. "Maybe the Department of Health
misinterpreted the law, but it definitely says any dog that is
menacing—it doesn't even have to bite anybody, it just has to be
menacing—can be removed. You might try reminding them of that."

I already had. A few minutes earlier, I had called Ed Boyce,
the head of the veterinary branch of the Department of Health,
and read him that law. There was no confusion: "I'm familiar with
it," he told me. "But we don't enforce it."

"Then who does enforce it?" After a long pause he said, "No
one enforces dog-to-dog laws."

"Wait a minute," I said. "So you're telling me there *is* a law
against what this pack is doing, but no one enforces it?"

His response: "That's correct."

Okay, I said, so how about going after the dogs because they
bite people? Nope, he told me; the people they bite don't count
because they were with dogs—the pack was probably going after
their dogs and the people just got in the way.

"So you're saying you'd rather wait until they maul a person?"

"That's what you're saying," he told me. "That's not what I'm
saying."

——————— 🦴 ———————

Elizabeth couldn't talk about the attack until weeks after it happened. She and Bonny had been walking down 36th Street when three of Harry's big brown and white hound dogs pushed open their junkyard's gate and charged. One grabbed Bonny by the head and lifted her off the sidewalk; the others took her hind legs and pulled in opposite directions. Elizabeth kicked the dogs and pounded their faces, yelling, "Somebody help—they're ripping her in half!" No one responded. Five other dogs ran from the junkyard and latched onto Bonny's face, tail, stomach, and throat. Harry eventually hobbled from behind the fence, saying, "Don't make trouble for me. I have a bad heart." Somehow Bonny slipped away, flying up 36th Street toward home, her body torn open and bleeding, with eight dogs on her tail. That's when she ran into the courtyard, where the pack cornered her until Ralphie came along with the two-by-four.

I replayed that scene in my head for weeks as I watched Harry's lot, hoping his dogs would get loose so I could call 911 like everyone said I should. But it didn't happen.

So instead, I called Channel 2, the local CBS affiliate. That night, the evening news showed pictures of Bonny after the attack and me lamenting the city's inaction. It showed the rickety latch on the junkyard and Harry saying the reason his dogs attacked Bonny was that "somebody opened the gate." Most importantly, it showed Harry standing in front of his lot, smirking, and saying this: "If somebody opens the gate by mistake, they might attack somebody else."

Still nothing changed. As Bonny began healing and needing to go outside four or five times a day, I walked the streets of Manhattan carrying a carving knife—exactly the kind I had used to cut dogs apart in the morgue. I clutched the handle, blade hardly hidden in my pocket, and walked the streets of midtown knowing that any second, six hundred pounds of dog could come tearing around a corner, ready to kill us. I walked along reviewing my dog anatomy, and I planned my routes based on where I could hide Bonny when the dogs came: *This* convenience store, *that* dumpster, the entryways of *those* apartment buildings.

I called the mayor's office again, the Community Board, the City Council, you name it. They told me they'd look into it and call back. They never did. People started saying I should sue Harry. But for what? His rusted hot dog carts? An injunction that would take years to get, and that he'd probably ignore? My neighbors told me to poison the dogs, but that wouldn't help anything: Harry'd just get more dogs, and I'd end up in jail.

So Harry's pack is still going strong. A few weeks ago, a neighbor told me they cornered a group of children playing in front of the Javits Center. They barked and lunged until people heard screams and ran them off. A few days later, they tore apart another dog and attacked its owner, Hal Caplin, who ended up in the emergency room with twelve stitches in his face. He called the Department of Health and the police and got the same old story. As have others. The *Times* recently ran an article about a group of neighbors on the East Side who've seen their dogs get attacked and beheaded by two rottweilers, but the city gives them the same "we don't do dog-on-dog" line they give me. Maybe I'll call them next, to see about challenging the city together.

So yes, I'm still obsessed with Harry and his dogs. I'm furious about what they did to Bonny, but this is about more than my dog. It's about the city needing to fix a law—and a law-enforcement problem. It's also about an autopsy I did ten years ago—an autopsy that still haunts me. It was on a rottweiler who mauled and killed a young girl outside Denver. The girl was playing on her swing when the dog lunged from behind and killed her. Ate her while her mother watched, screaming from the kitchen window. During the autopsy, I had to sort through that dog's stomach and take inventory: one long blond braid with scalp attached. One child's ear. That dog had a history of mauling other dogs. Just like the Florida pack that killed eighty-one-year-old Alice Broom in her front yard days before Bonny's attack. They'd terrorized Alice's neighborhood for months, attacking people, mauling other dogs. Neighbors complained endlessly to authorities but got nowhere.

A few weeks ago, as Bonny and I walked up 9th Avenue with my boyfriend, David, I saw four of Harry's dogs trotting toward us. They were two blocks away, weaving through pedestrians during rush hour. Harry was a good half-block behind the dogs. Bonny didn't see them; if she had, she'd have been gone. Because here's the thing: After months of nursing, she walks and runs just fine. She may never regain full use of one hind leg, but other than that she's okay, physically. Mentally is another story. She recently started wrestling with me again, but full contact terrifies her. And dog barks send her into a panic—she screams and flails, struggles to escape her collar or bite through her leash to run home. So when I saw Harry's dogs coming toward us, I handed David the leash. "Those are the dogs," I said. "Take her across the street."

As David and Bonny crossed 9th Avenue, I stood in the middle of the sidewalk, facing Harry's dogs, watching them run toward me. And I did what every city official said to do when I saw them loose: I called 911.

"Are they attacking anyone right now?" the dispatcher asked.

"No."

"Sorry," she told me. "Try Animal Control." I called Animal Control, the Department of Health, and the mayor's office. I talked to a traffic cop, then called 911 again. Guess what they said? "Are they attacking anyone right now?"

"No," I said, as Harry's dogs ran past me toward the junkyard. "Would you rather wait until they do?"

Seven Reasons Not to Get a Dog

Marion Winik

1. **Your aesthetic standards will collapse.**
At the beginning of every creative writing class I
teach, I forbid students to write about their pets. This rule is
never well received. They eye me balefully as I list the dangers of
predictability and sentimentality and, along similar lines, ask any
grandmothers present to avoid the topic of their grandchildren.
Then, after about a week away from home in rainy Pittsburgh
this past January, having just made the no-pets speech to a new
crop of students, my coat began to smell unmistakably and
heartbreakingly of the puppy we had just gotten for Christmas.
I dashed off some sentences on the back of an envelope, then
crumpled it in horror.

2. You will lose interest in humanity.

You probably do not imagine that you will prefer the dog to all
the other living creatures with whom you regularly associate. But
you will. No one is more loving, less demanding, more forgiving,
more cuddly. No one is sorrier when wrong, no one makes a more
abject show of it, and no one is more overjoyed to be forgiven.
"You love Beau more than me," moans my little daughter, and
my husband does not correct her. Like the three cats to whom I
also used to give a fair amount of attention, he simply watches
through slitted eyes.

3. You will steal from your children.

"It's not even going to be my dog!" I told those who objected, who
said I was nuts to get a puppy, what with my preexisting group
of teenagers, toddlers, animals, and philosophers, all having to
be fed and cared for. See, I wasn't getting a dog for me; I was
giving my sixteen-year-old son, Hayes, a dog for Christmas. I
searched on the Internet until I found a likely vendor of miniature
dachshunds in the nearby town of Dillsburg, Pennsylvania, and I
sneaked off with my other son to see the puppies when they were
just six weeks old. They were all male, and the smallest one had a
large scar across the top of his head. This is the one Vince selected
immediately, to the breeder's surprise. She assured us the vet had

said it would eventually disappear. Actually, it has only gotten more pronounced, but of course we do not care.

4. In naming dogs, we all stand naked.

I drove back to Discount Dachshunds of Dillsburg, as I had come to think of it, with Hayes on Christmas Eve. He was moved by the gift (even though I knew he thought the "life-changing" present I'd teased him about was a car), and he immediately suggested naming his tiny new pet after his father, who died when he was six. That was a moment I will not forget. This boy shut down so hard at the time of his dad's death, he did not cry about it then or since. And yet I had to try to explain to him why giving the dog his father's name wouldn't be okay. I could just picture his grandmother, my late husband's mom, coming for a visit: "And this our new dog, Tony." Honestly, I couldn't handle it either. Instead, the dog is named Beau, which was one of his dad's nicknames, and this sleek and sociable ladies' man, this solicitous ten-pound face-licker, this equal-opportunity lover of children and delivery men and cats wears it well.

5. Can your fragile psyche really take more neurotic terror?

Every so-still heap of fur in the road stops your breath, fills your eyes, lumps your throat. It is a groundhog, it is a rabbit, it is a kitten, it is not your dog, but it is small and dead and it is close enough. (If you are a parent, you are already familiar with a parallel phenomenon, the way any dead child is always, for at least one moment, yours.) No matter how much dead animals have always bothered you, it is much worse when you have the terrible

Beau

brevity of the canine lifespan on your mind. Even my son goes through this. For example, the other day we were discussing how great things will be when I turn sixty-two-and-a-half and can collect my IRAs. That will be fifteen years from now, he quickly calculated. Will Beau be alive then?

6. You can forget about Paris,
   Johnny Depp, Thai food.

This is what I'm trying to tell you. They live just one year for every seven of ours, and that is the best-case scenario. Perhaps this is why you will love your dog seven times as much as a human being. You won't want go out to dinner, you won't go to the movies, and you will make up excuses to avoid international travel. Instead you will take your dog to the park, or perhaps to a therapist, a summer camp, a spa. A doggie diner, a poochie playdate, a puppy kindergarten. No matter, you will not be embarrassed. *Surely people have always loved their dogs this much,* that is what I tell myself, and you will too.

7. You'll lose your dignity.

The heat of him, the smell (a lady at the tire shop told me the other day, "Smell behind their ears, they always smell just like a puppy behind the ears," and she bent to bury her face in his neck, and because I take him almost everywhere with me I have conversations like this with strangers all the time), the soft fur of his paws, his long, delicate muzzle, his droopy velvet ears, his winsome markings, his round dark eyes. A dachshund burrows deep under your covers to sleep at your feet, and as soon as you wake in the middle of the night because the boys did not come home, or because the boys did come home, or because someone is vomiting in the bathroom, or because it was that dream, that dream again, you feel immediately for the warm fur, the beating heart, your loyal friend, your baby. Listen to me: If you value your self-respect, your family, your career, and the dignity of your species, don't get a dog.

Orange Snarly Magic
Jennifer Sexton

We met by chance at the dog kennel. It was my summer job.

I was eighteen. She was two. I was a vegetarian. She was an enthusiastic omnivore. I had a pierced nose. She had a spay scar. Perfect matches like these happen once in a lifetime, if you're lucky. Tanny Bananny and I were that lucky.

First her white slash of smile swam to me out of the darkness. Then a small background satellite bouncing back and forth, left and right in the gloom—the arcing white tip of a tail. My eyes adjusted from the blazing Cape Cod August outside to the sour, timeless dim of the kennel's cement interior. I took the ever-present Bayview Boarding Kennels leash from its place around my neck and opened the latch of kennel #19. So this was the skinny, bat-eared mixed breed that my coworker had barely snatched that morning from needless euthanasia during a chance visit to the vet clinic. This was the waif we were now harboring and trying to find a home for. The scrawled name card on the kennel door read simply: TANNY.

I expected her to be tan. She was. I expected fear, distrust, anxiety in the pointy little fox face. She had all of that. What I didn't expect was the naked hope there, the unmistakable question. "Are you *her*? You're *her*, aren't you?" she asked me with every ligament of her taut body.

"Tanny, huh? You're gonna need more name than that. I can see that right away. You're more orange than tan, anyway. You're a special girl, aren't you? Yes, you are! How about . . . Tangerine? Tangerine Banana? You like that? We can still call you Tanny for short. Tanny Bananny."

I didn't yet know as I slipped the leash around her throat that I was stepping permanently into the spotlight of a wild and bewildering love. I was a kid. I didn't know what taking sole responsibility for another life meant. I was hardly capable of my own care and feeding. I wasn't looking for a dog, but that didn't matter. I was *her*. I was *hers*. And she was mine.

Within a few days, I stopped walking prospective adoptive families back to kennel #19 to size up the scrawny orange orphan who seemed to either snarl and lunge toward or cringe away trembling from every human who approached. Every human except me.

I whisked my small orange cohort away during lunch breaks, two smiling escapees leaping into my beat-up hatchback and roaring out onto Historic Route 6A with the music cranked. I sang along to the Violent Femmes or the Smiths as Tanny snapped her jaws at the hot sea wind, her ears like twin sails bearing us nobly to the Burger King drive-through window. "The usual," I'd chirp. I ate my vegetarian special—large fries and a chocolate shake—seated behind the wheel in the beach parking lot. Tanny nibbled her cheeseburger delicately—not at all the desperate wolfing you'd expect from such a hardscrabble little survivor. These were undoubtedly her first cheeseburgers, but she must have sensed somehow that there were many more to come. When all fast food wrappers were duly emptied and squished into delicious-smelling balls of greasy paper, we chased each other around in the sand for the remainder of our thirty minutes of freedom. Our lighthearted romps generally ended with my desperately pulling Tanny's twenty enraged pounds off some unsuspecting beachcomber or his dog, but we didn't let their intrusions or expletives cast a shadow over our outings.

By the end of the week I decided to take her home with me

for good. Tanny, ever vigilant, seemed to believe on a molecular level that only in my presence was she secure enough to safely let her guard down. When I liberated her from kennel #19 at

Tanny

the end of my shift that day, her ears relaxed from their stiff triangles into gentle folds of velvet and her high arc of a tail wilted into a natural half-mast curve. Her eyes softened and her smile was comically, tragically, human in its expression of frank relief. I did not deserve the trust of this creature. I had done nothing to earn the faith she had in me. She curled into an orange spiral on the passenger seat as we rode home in and out of lengthening shadows, her tail neatly cradling her sleeping face.

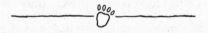

Tanny's been gone for two years. I'm wandering the California beach, losing myself in the rhythmic roll and retreat of the waves, when a guy arrives with his dog. Not just any dog. Not another floppy-eared Lab or anti-gravity Jack Russell or blur-footed, trotting dachshund, not a ubiquitous, bandanna'd shepherd mix. This dog's silhouette clicks into a spot left vacant years ago by

Tanny's departure from my side and from this earth. I have a small, pointy, orange, empty spot in my retinas that tries to fill itself with the shapes of dogs. They never quite fit. But when one does come along with that certain ratio of barrel chest to greyhound-lean waist, that banner of fox tail held just so, that pointy face framed with bat ears, the click of that shape neatly fitting into my dog-shaped emptiness is practically audible. And I simply must ask.

"Excuse me—I'm in love with your dog. What kind is she?"

Since I never met the sorry excuses for human beings who dropped Tanny at the vet clinic to barely escape being euthanized, I was never able to find out what mix of breeds she was. What kinds of dogs in what proportions created that scrappy, perfect little dog's body?

"Oh, he's corgi and whippet."

"She's a Labra-huahua."

"We don't know. A mutt. Heinz 57—ha, ha, ha!"

Somehow I feel that if I can just figure out what dogs she was made up of, I will hold some key to her existence that will bring her closer to me, even in death. I could write the breeds and their percentages on an index card and carry it next to my heart—the recipe for the first and wildest love of my life—on the off chance that I might someday find myself in the right kitchen with the right ingredients to bring Tanny Bananny forth again, warm with life, from some mystical oven.

"Oh. I used to have a dog that looked like him. Sort of. Now that I see him more clearly, her face was sharper. And her fur was more . . . fluffy. No, no, the bone structure's all wrong. Too friendly, too. Needs more snarl. Well, thanks anyway."

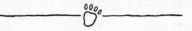

Tanny's been gone almost six years. I'm walking past an outdoor café in Pendleton, Oregon, when I feel another pronounced *click*. A gray-bearded man is sitting, sipping coffee and gazing out into the street. Across the table from him, a Tanny lookalike sits in the other white wrought-iron chair, looking like she owns the joint and half the block in either direction. She raises one lip slightly, silently, at my approach. I smile.

"Hi—I'm in love with your dog. I used to have one a lot like her."

"Oh, thank you, Miss."

"I'm no Miss anymore! I'm a Mrs.—or a Ms. I'm just meeting up with my husband and baby daughter. Here they come now."

"Well, best keep your little girl clear. This here's no kid's dog."

"Oh? That right? Scrappy, is she? Aw, that's sweet. My dog was like that too. What mix is she, anyway?"

"Oh, she's not a mix of anything. She's pure dingo."

"A dingo! But what . . . where . . . why do you have a pet dingo? In Oregon? Is that legal?"

"Well, I don't know about legal, and as far as the authorities know, she's a fox terrier, if you get my meaning, Miss, er, Ma'am."

"Well, where did you get her?"

"I was camping a few years ago in the New Mexico desert, sitting there under the stars, and I noticed a ring of little eyes shining in the dark, in a circle around me and my campfire. Well, I thought they were coyotes, and I started stomping and hollering, and they all scattered. All except one. She crept up and started taking some hot dogs from my hands, and, well, when I woke up the next morning she was still curled up there right in front of my tent flap. Figured she was taking me on permanent. So I took her home."

"And they were really dingos? What, a pack of Australian dingos found their way to New Mexico? What were you, near Roswell or something?"

"Guy at the gas station told me there's a pack of 'em out there living on the rabbits and whatever they find. Nobody knows how they got there. It's a lot like Australia out there, I guess. And there they are, explanation or no explanation."

Hmm. I like the idea of Tanny being a dingo from New Mexico. It's magical. Exotic. But still, it isn't quite right. This one's a bit too

muscly. Too butch looking. Too coarse. Not fragile enough. Not soft
and deerlike enough. Not quite like delicate Tanny Bananny.

———————— 🐾 ————————

Tanny has been gone eight years this summer. She left the world
peacefully after a blessedly short illness, silver faced and frail.
I still hardly believe she's gone. I can't go to the beach without
thinking of her, feeling her racing around me in the sand, young
again, an orange streak of light just ahead of my field of vision as
I whirl to find her. My husband and I are stretched on a blanket,
enjoying a picnic dinner at Golden Gardens Beach near our home
in Seattle. The sun is enormous and blood red as it slides behind
the plum-colored Olympic Mountains. The little brown-eyed force
of nature who orbits our blanket at about knee height, kicking
up tiny sandstorms and darting in for the occasional bite of food,
is not Tanny but our one-and-a-half-year-old daughter, Ava. The
evening is pure in its perfection, with dozens of pale sailboats on
the darkening water and a fellow picnicker's shared soundscape of
random pop music. The setting is heavy with beauty. It presses us
into the sand.

"Dog! Dog!" says Ava, pointing to the paved path separating
the beach from the grassy picnic area. I turn to follow her
gesture, and it happens. *Click.*

"Excuse me! I'm in love with your dog," I cry to the young man. His face breaks into a smile, perfectly echoed in the face of his pointy orange dog. I remember that smile. The smile of coconspirators.

"Thanks! Me too!" he gushes. The dog races toward the waves, recoils the instant a toe touches water, and rushes a resting seagull, who, caught off guard, bursts upward in a confused flap and nearly crashes into a woman's face. She shrieks. "Sorry," calls the smiling man, with a noticeable lack of concern. The apology flies out of his mouth with ease. He has said this word many, many times.

"Does she like kids?" I ask, corralling Ava with both hands, balancing my picnic plate between them.

"If by 'like' you mean likes to bite 'em, she sure does!" he crows. "Ha ha!"

Tanny used to snarl in the general direction of toddlers. I found it charming. I had yet to become a parent myself, and I didn't see what the fuss was about. She was wild! Spirited! Sassy! My attitude earned me a Thanksgiving dinner eaten balanced on my knees in the basement of my dad's girlfriend's condo the one year I was invited there for a holiday, after Tanny tried to sample the plump drumstick of a young relative and we were both banished.

"What about cheeseburgers? She like cheeseburgers?" I ask.

"You kidding me? I can't even say the C-word or she goes insane! I have to spell it or she knows what I mean and won't settle down until we go through the Burger King drive-through!"

"Wow. She reminds me so much of my own dog. My . . . late dog." This just might be it. This dog looks enough like Tanny to be her twin, and her personality fits the profile perfectly. I may be about to learn the secret of my dog's identity, the recipe for the dearly departed Tanny Bananny. I am almost afraid to ask.

"So . . . do you know what kind of dog she is?"

"Yup. She's half dingo and half Australian cattle dog."

Hmm. This might be the answer. My heart both rises and sinks. It's thrilling and strangely anticlimactic.

"Australian, huh? So how did she end up here in Seattle? I know she didn't swim seven thousand miles," I say, pointing at the dog, now snarling and snapping at the very ocean itself.

"Nope. She hates water. I don't know how she got here. I guess it was magic."

I knew it. This is it. Tanny Bananny came from the other side of the planet, half loyal dog and half wild animal, by means of some orange, snarly canine magic to give me the gift of being her hero.

"What's your dog's name?" I ask the guy. He smiles and looks a bit sheepish.

"Her name is Sprocket the Big Red Rocket," he says, laughing. "She's not a big dog, but she's not your run of the mill Ginger or Lady. She needed a lot of name."

"I know exactly what you mean," I say, cuddling my daughter and watching Sprocket the Big Red Rocket dashing toward the water and rolling back like a canine wave, sprinting and dancing and spinning on her toes in the rich russet air of an August dusk.

Looking for Dave
Jill Rothenberg

Dave, the first man in my dog, Otie's, life, made a big first impression. So much so that in the six years after we broke up, all it took was the sight of a man driving a truck to get Otie's attention.

But not just any man. Although Otie wasn't particularly picky about the size or make of the truck (though he preferred older-model, half- or three-quarter-ton Fords), he had certain criteria about the man driving it: They had to be as much like Dave as possible, which was a tall order. Kind, good-natured, intelligent, funny, a bit rough around the edges but still boyishly handsome, with his wild days (mostly) behind him. Bonus points if he was wearing Carhartts, a tool belt, and a baseball hat.

The truth is—surprise—these were really my preferences.

Otie, as a high-strung, only-child weimaraner, had become my matchmaker, desperate to pair me off with someone who would bring some much-needed male companionship into our lives. He missed the energy, the action, the roughhousing, the testosterone high he got when he was around men and not stuck in our estrogen chamber of an apartment. He longed for a guy to wrestle with him on the floor, to chase him around the yard. "Hey, buddy," Dave would say as he scratched behind Otie's ears, and Otie would cock his head to the side and close his eyes, in doggy heaven. "How you doin', boy?"

No matter that I did these things already. They just weren't the same. When I got down on the floor and pulled on his paws and tried to get him to play, he'd give me a bored look and turn away and then look back at me with a curious expression, like I was trying to talk to him in another language. And I was. Man-speak. Problem was, I wasn't fluent.

It didn't matter where we were. We could be stopped in traffic, or trying to find a parking spot at Safeway, or just driving down the street, but if we saw a truck with a close-enough approximation of Dave, Otie, who always rode shotgun, would turn quickly to the window, jump up on the armrest, and stick his elegant-yet-goofy weimaraner face out the window. His ears would be in full perk-up mode, his tale would be wagging a mile a minute, and sometimes he would even let loose with a friendly bark. Being the over-worried dog mom that I was, I imagined that he was really saying, *Please take me away in the back of your truck to the promised land of tug-of-war, endless Frisbee marathons, the nonstop adventure of construction sites, and the delicious cuisine of roach coaches. And you'd like my mom. Can she come, too?*

Walking around our neighborhoods and local parks, in Denver and Boulder, Otie always had his radar tuned to the man-driving-pickup frequency. We would be walking along and I would be preoccupied, going over what I needed to pick up at the Wild Oats Market near our apartment in downtown Denver, when I would feel a tug on the leash. More often than not, it was a truck driving by or better yet, a parked truck. On a recent road trip we stopped for the night at a motel in Rawlins, Wyoming. There in the parking lot was Otie's dream come true: a long row of contractors' trucks, all different sizes and colors, some with the ubiquitous orange water containers in the back, some with camper shells, but all with the same magical effect.

As I unloaded my duffel bug and Otie's gear from the trunk, he sniffed around at a few nearby trucks, homing in on the driver's side doors as he always did. Sometimes this truck obsession would break my heart. I felt like a terrible dog mom for making my sweetheart of a dog suffer without his dad. More often than not, though, I could see the humor in it. There, in a windy, truck-filled motel parking lot in the middle of nowhere, I had to laugh. Instead of waiting at the front door for his master, here was Otie waiting patiently by a stranger's truck, expecting that Dave would slide down out of the cab, rub his neck, and say, "Hey, boy."

Otie

Otie had always followed Dave around like Dave was the Pied Piper. If we were both at home, Otie would most likely be with Dave—in the backyard while he mowed the grass, hanging around the garage while he worked on his truck, or downstairs in the woodshop. Did he want to lie with me as I read a book? Or go with me in the car? Maybe play with one of his toys? No. He was a guy dog and wanted to do manly dog things.

Like all weimaraners, Otie was sensitive, dramatic, and needy, though much more so with me, it seemed. We made a good pair. After Dave and I broke up, Otie and I went through a period of readjustment, getting to know each other again after nearly seven years of living in a testosterone-tempered world where it often felt like he was more Dave's dog than mine. When we got our own place, we were like two best friends getting reacquainted after years of being apart. We truly became partners then, sleeping side by side on the bed, cuddling in the morning, and going absolutely everywhere together in my Subaru.

Post-Dave, he was as obsessed with me as I was with him, following me from room to room of our apartment, sitting on my lap on the couch (he weighed seventy pounds), and waiting patiently on the bath mat outside the shower until I slid the curtain open to see his mournful, concerned face. It made me sad, because I knew he was looking for Dave.

Dave is a carpenter, contractor, and mechanic—truly a jack-of-all-trades. He's got an ease about him, a way of making people feel at home, like nothing bad will happen as long as he's around. Or if it does, he'll deal with it. The joke among our friends was always that Dave would outlast any contestant on *Survivor*. That's not to say he wouldn't drive you crazy like anyone else, but you wouldn't lack for food, shelter—or entertainment, for that matter.

Otie was only seven months old when I met Dave on Valentine's Day night at the Little Bear, a bar in Evergreen, Colorado, near where I was living at the time. I had gone with my married friends Marsha and Terry, who were fellow weimaraner owners (Terry, in fact, was Otie's vet). Emboldened by a few drinks, I approached Dave, who was sitting with a friend, and asked him to dance. As a proud new dog mom, one of the first things

I mentioned, yelling over the crowded and noisy bar, was that I had a dog—a weimaraner. Dave nodded and later told me that he thought I said rottweiler. He came over a few days later, his pickup bouncing up the nearly impassable road leading up to my house. When Otie shot out the front door, I saw Dave's surprised expression as he said, "Oh, no, you have one of *those* dogs."

One time, in the early months of our relationship, we left Otie in Dave's brother's brand-new house in Gunnison while we went skiing. When we returned, we found that Otie not only had chewed through the drywall in the garage and gnawed into the tough fiberglass of a ski, but also had left the hugest piles of poop I had ever seen in the living room and the guest room. I was mortified—here I was with my new boyfriend in his brother's beautiful, immaculate mountain home (and whose golden retriever was one of the most mellow and well behaved I have ever met), and my dog had done not only structural but unmistakably stinky damage as well. After all that, Dave was sweet and reassuring. "C'mon, babe, he's a dog. It's no big deal. We'll clean it up and just take him with us next time." So we did.

Another time, Dave wasn't quite as understanding. We were in Gunnison with a group of his friends (and Otie, of course) and had hiked into an area known for its excellent fishing. They were looking forward to fishing; I was looking forward to reading the book I had brought. They had set up their lines with patience, precision, and an enthusiasm that I could never quite comprehend, which is why I had learned to bring a book. We had to be quiet, so the fish wouldn't hear or see us through the crystal-clear water. All the lines were set, and it was a beautiful, quiet, sunny morning with only the sound of birds chirping. We were all enjoying how peaceful and relaxing it was when all of a sudden, I heard a big splash and then a chorus of angry voices: "Goddamnit, damned dog, get the hell out of here." And then Dave, "Damnit, Otie, get over here, Jesus." It turns out that Otie, who loved to swim, had decided to get a running start behind us where we couldn't see him. Dave said he heard a rustling in the grass and the next thing he knew, he looked up to see Otie midflight over the beaver pond, ears flapping in the air like Dumbo as he fell smack in the middle of the fishing lines that had been set so carefully. He was loving life, treading around in the water, but pulling the lines all over the place. There would be no fish for dinner that night.

Hiking back to the car, with a wet and joyous Otie at our side, I felt sheepish. "Sorry," I kept saying. Dave said not to worry about it, but I could tell he wasn't thrilled with Otie's performance. "You can't let him do whatever he wants, hon," he said, as if I had any control whatsoever over Otie at that point. He was right, though. I had tried to discipline Otie, but he never listened. Dave had taken on the role of disciplinarian, tough and patient at the same time. And it worked: The longer we were together, the better behaved Otie became.

Although I knew he was fond of Otie and had always been a dog lover, Dave's tough-love campaign took some getting used to. Soon after we moved in together, though, I admitted that Otie could stand to learn a basic command or two. I enrolled us in a puppy training class. But we didn't exactly pass with flying colors: Otie and I only lasted a few classes, until we were asked to leave, since we were labeled "slow" by the instructor and accused of holding back the rest of the class.

It was the "stay" command that did us in. This command was a challenge for both of us, mainly because it required us to be apart—even if it was only twenty feet. I would take my place in the line of other dog owners, facing our dogs. After instructing our dogs to stay, we would first walk in a circle around them, repeating "stay," like a mantra, and then turn our backs and walk a very short distance and stop, where we would turn around again. Presumably, the dogs would still be in the "stay" position and happy to see our approving faces. But Otie and I never got past the part where I walked in a circle around him. Instead, he would break formation and cry, trying to jump up on me. I tried to be serious and get him to act like the other dogs, but it was funny and I would laugh. Or I would get irritated. No matter what my reaction was, one thing was clear: It wasn't working.

A few weeks later, Dave and I decided to go the home-schooling route. We would walk around the trail that runs along the creek in the mountain town of Kittredge where we lived, telling Otie to "stay" as we walked ahead, our backs to him. "Don't look back," Dave would say, but I couldn't resist. I wouldn't even be half-turned around when Otie would run up to me with such excitement that his legs would seem to be going in four different directions, his tail wagging furiously. Dave would sigh, exasperated. "He's never going to learn, hon." But he'd be laughing, too. Otie's weimaraner face—that particular blend of dead-serious composure about to give way to utter chaos so characteristic of the breed—cracked us up every time.

We had an equally hard time getting him to ride in the bed of the truck, rather than in the cab with us. I was worried that he would fall out somehow, or be carried away by a strong wind. Of course, at nearly eight months old, he was a big boy and was in no danger of going anywhere. Dave said he would learn how to steady himself in the back, that all dogs did, and that it wasn't like we were driving in the Indy 500.

Otie would start out in the back, adjusting himself to the motion of the truck, ears flapping in the wind, and didn't look at all happy to be there. It was like getting him to learn "stay"; I knew I shouldn't turn around and look at him because when I did, he would want to be with us. "I'm keeping an eye on him," Dave would say, looking in the rearview mirror. But he would be laughing. That would cause me to turn around, and there Otie would be, his face pressed against the glass of the window that separates the truck bed from the cab, willing his way into the comfort of snuggling between us. Dave or I would slide the window open, and it was never fast enough. Otie would already have his front paws on its thin ledge and would push his head through so he was halfway in. We would reach out and pull him in, where he would settle in between us with a contented sigh.

His "roughing it" in the back of the truck officially came to an end, though, after we left him there one day when we stopped at the store. I had my hands full with things to put in the shopping cart when I heard a voice over the loudspeaker, "There's a weimaraner in the parking lot; there's a weimaraner in the parking lot. Please come get your weimaraner." Dave said later that I dropped everything and hurried up the aisle. I don't remember anything, except thinking that it was a busy Saturday afternoon and there were a lot of cars in the parking lot. I had visions of Otie motionless on the pavement. When I got outside, cars were stopped in both directions and Otie was looking around, confused and trying to find us. I rushed up to him, got him out of the cars' way, and hugged him again and again. We still laugh about the parking lot incident, especially the announcement on the loudspeaker, but at the time it was scary. His days of riding in the back were over.

When Dave and I broke up in January 2000, after nearly seven years together, we remained good friends and continued to see each other regularly. Otie came with me in the move from Golden to Denver, and Olive, whom we had adopted together, stayed with Dave. Deciding to move to the Bay Area in January 2005 for a job was a tough decision. I had been downsized from my job in Boulder and wanted to stay in my field, but the job market didn't look good and showed no immediate signs of improving. Moving meant leaving my friends, including Dave, and starting again in a new place. I was thirty-eight; Otie was twelve. We weren't exactly spring chickens. But I was moving for a good reason, and it would be an adventure. Plus, as my friends reassured me, everyone would come visit and I was only a short flight away. And Otie and I had each other. We would be doing this together.

When we arrived in Oakland, Otie did his best to sniff out the right men, or at least those closest to what he was used to: rugged, Carhartt-wearing, truck-driving carpenters and contractors. I think he was trying to gain some sort of equilibrium himself, to surround himself with the familiarity and comfort of home. And luckily, one of these men couldn't have been closer—my next-door neighbor Chris (who, in one of those strange but true coincidences, has a black Lab named Otis). Chris and I became fast friends, and I felt lucky to have such a sweetheart living next door. Chris is a beautiful guy inside and out, a dream come true for Otie in his Carhartt work pants, tool belt, and baseball hat. Otie loved going to Chris's to get his testosterone fix, as Chris and I dished about anything and everything going on in our lives. We would be the perfect couple, we joke, if Chris were straight. The fact that he's not has probably made us closer. To make matters even better, he's had a soft spot for Otie since day one. He and Otie would play with a toy, or a bone, and Otie would strut around with his tail straight out, a sure sign that he was happily back in familiar territory.

We had only been in Oakland a few months when another man was detected by Otie's I-think-he-may-be-good-for-me-and-my-mom radar. We were on an after-work walk near my apartment when I heard a guy call down from a balcony above. "Hey, nice weimaraner. Can I come down and say hi?" He was just our type—very handsome in a rough-around-the-edges sort of way, with a warm smile and intensely blue eyes. He was standing next to a woman with bleached blond hair, who held up a small, pouffy white dog in way of introduction. I thought they were your standard

Lake Merritt couple, this neighborhood in Oakland being far and away the most eccentric place I've ever lived. But Otie's intent gaze upward indicated that yes, we would like for him to come down and say hello, though there wasn't a truck in sight. Jerry and Otie became fast friends as he introduced himself and hunkered down on his knees to playfully rub Otie's head and scratch behind his ears. *Uh-oh,* Otie seemed to say as he looked up at me, *we may have a winner here.* But I figured, nah, he may be our type, but he's also most likely taken—I mean, what's with the blond?

We didn't see Jerry again for a few months, until one day when we were on a walk and saw him on the sidewalk, working on a motorcycle. Otie instantly came to life. The walk had been ho-hum until this point, but upon seeing Jerry, the tail-wagging kicked into high gear and he pulled me over to where Jerry knelt in front of his Harley. "How's your dog?" I asked, thinking that the white puffball dog didn't really match his biker persona. "What dog?" he answered, looking perplexed. It turns out that he had been staying with his friend (not a girlfriend, he emphasized more than once) while he was moving into another place down the block, only a block away from where I live. Otie and I weren't sure whether he was just friendly neighborhood guy or whether he might like us, package deal that we were. It would be another month before we'd meet again.

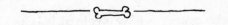

During this time, after we had only been in Oakland four months, Otie started to visibly slow down. He couldn't walk as far without resting and sometimes even turned around on a walk, signaling that he wanted to go home. When he started limping in March 2005, I thought he had pulled something and didn't take him to the vet right away, figuring that his leg might get better on its own. But a week later it was no better, so I took him to his vet in Berkeley. The vet looked troubled when he examined the leg and soon after took Otie away for x-rays.

He was gone a long time before he returned alone. "I'm afraid I have bad news," he said. I was numb. *What could be wrong?* I thought. "I think Otie has cancer in his leg, and that's what's causing him to limp." I don't remember much, except looking at the x-ray that clearly showed the mass on his leg. A chest x-ray showed a mass on Otie's heart as well, and a few days later I met with the oncologist who confirmed the diagnosis of osteosarcoma, or bone cancer. He thought Otie might have anywhere from eight weeks to a few months to live. Because of his age and his arthritis, which had also gotten worse, I decided to treat him with medication and make him as comfortable as possible.

He was the same old dog for a while, which allowed me

to enter my denial stage and pretend everything was going to be okay; the limp wasn't as pronounced, he still liked to go everywhere with me, and his huge appetite was intact.

During this time, Dave and I talked often, about all the good times with Otie, and also about our disbelief that he wasn't always going to be the same dog we knew and loved. I think we both had a hard time facing the fact that Otie wouldn't live forever, since he had been such a big part of our lives. I couldn't contemplate it. Otie was my organizing factor, my constant companion, the center of my universe.

When he started limping again four months later, in August, I was immediately concerned. And as we expected, Otie had another cancerous growth: One of his toes would have to be amputated. I decided to take him back to Terry in Colorado, where we could be among close friends, and especially with Dave.

Taking a road trip back to Colorado was a good tonic for both of us (including that stop at the Rawlins motel, complete with all the contractor trucks), and the surgery to remove the toe went better than expected. By the time we got back to Oakland, Otie seemed okay, though a bit more tired than usual. Around this time, Otie and I ran into Jerry again, and he invited both of us to a party he was having. Walking up the street to his house, Otie was pulling gently on the leash, as if to say, *C'mon, this time we're going to make an impression.* And Otie was right; we began to spend more time with Jerry, and it seemed like Otie's radar was still in good working order. But as soon as his matchmaking job was over, Otie's health took a bad turn.

Over the next two weeks, Otie had more and more trouble getting up on the bed or couch, didn't want to go outside as much, and gradually stopped eating. First he would eat a bit of his favorites, like peanut butter, bagels, and plain McDonald's hamburgers. But then he stopped eating, started losing weight, and was withdrawing from me, even when I tried to cuddle him. A short walk now wore him out.

One night, as we were lying on the bed, he started breathing hard and fast. I knew something was really wrong and rushed him to the vet. Jerry, who had taken care of his ailing Rhodesian Ridgeback during a long illness before finally making the difficult decision to put him to sleep, came with me. After examining him, the vet on duty said his heart was surrounded by fluid, which was making it hard for him to breathe. The only way he could regain his breath was if they drained the fluid.

After the procedure, he was breathing much easier the next day, though he was still lethargic and wouldn't eat. I was on the phone with my vet in Berkeley and Terry in Colorado every day for the next few days, as Otie seemed to be going downhill. Though my vet in Berkeley talked about different exploratory procedures to see if this was cancer related, Terry disagreed. He told me that exploratory procedures, besides being costly, would not improve the quality of Otie's life. In fact, he said, it could make it worse. "Having any kind of procedure at this point won't make him want to walk around in the park like he used to, or enjoy food the way he used to, or want to be an energetic guy the way he used to. You don't want to prolong his life if he's clearly suffering. You've given him an amazing life, and he deserves to go out with dignity. I've made the mistake with a few of my own dogs of prolonging their lives when they were suffering and I thought I was doing the right thing. I wasn't." My vet in Berkeley told me that the sac around Otie's heart would probably fill up with fluid again and again, but there was the outside chance that it wouldn't. And though they could continue to drain it, it could be a daily or weekly procedure, which would make Otie even weaker.

Only two days later, Otie's breathing became labored again. I didn't think it would happen again so fast. As I drove to the vet, I called Terry, I called Dave, I called my mom, I called Jerry. I just didn't want Otie to suffer anymore. I wanted him to be peaceful and content. I had always thought I would do anything—at all—to prolong his life. But the talk with Terry had touched me deeply. I loved my dog more than anything or anyone, and I didn't want to think about letting him go. But the thought of him suffering was worse.

Otie died later that night. I lay next to him on the floor with my face next to his, watching his beautiful, peaceful face. I had called Dave in Otie's last moments, and he cried, wishing so much that he could be with us. And he was in spirit. I told Otie that Dave was on the phone when he was still conscious and breathing hard, and I like to think that he heard me.

When I go back to Colorado during the Christmas holiday, I will take Otie's ashes with me. I'm not sure where I will take them—there are so many places that he found joy and doggy nirvana with Dave and me. But I'm thinking it might be at that spot outside Gunnison where he did a cannonball into the fishing lines with such glee and abandon. I think he'd like that.

My Dog Speaks English

Maria Goodavage

It all started innocently enough. One day when my daughter was about six years old, she had a cold and was resting on the couch next to our big yellow Lab, Jake. He planted his head on her lap, looked at her tenderly, and sighed.

"Oh, Jake, I love you!" Laura snuffled through her tissues at Jake's display of sympathy. Suddenly, a voice that sounded like Winnie the Pooh on female hormones replied, "I love you too, Laura." It was the first time Jake had said anything recognizably English besides the occasional *roof*-sounding bark. But neither of us was really surprised by his utterance. He'd always struck us as a rather intelligent dog. "Oh, Jakey," Laura cooed, stroking his head while getting back to the book she'd been perusing. I padded off to the kitchen to prepare lunch.

A few days later, Laura was having trouble deciding which sweater to wear. We were running late and it was cold, and no coaxing from me would convince her to wear her thick wool sweater.

Then Jake piped up in his odd little voice, "You should wear the wool one!"

"Okay!" she replied, and without a moment's hesitation slipped it on.

After a while, Jake's helpful hints began extending to homework. I'd ask Laura a math problem like, "What's two plus three?" If she were getting frustrated trying to figure it out, Jake would interject from the couch, "It's a number!" She'd giggle, and suddenly her mindblock was gone. "Five!" she'd exclaim. "Thank you, Jake." "Not a problem, Laura." And the math would flow.

At first Jake's little comments were limited to Laura. But one evening Jake brought my husband into his loquacious fold. Craig had heard Jake speak to Laura a few times, but he'd never been on the receiving end of the conversation.

Craig and I were eating dinner and discussing which movie to see that night. I had my heart set on a classic comedy at an old red-velvety cinema. Craig pined for an action flick at a plastic cineplex. Jake, who happened to be on plate-watch vigil for this meal, piped up with a suggestion. "You know how Maria gets about boy movies! C'mon, just go to the Castro Theatre and see the comedy already!"

As if he had been spoken to by a fellow human being, Craig calmly looked at his dog and replied, "All right, Jake. You win." This made Jake happy. "Good decision!" he said, never breaking his plate-mongering gaze.

Jake's English fluency has also proved helpful in matters involving household repairs. I'd been asking Craig to fix a very leaky tub faucet for months. The leak was getting so bad that Laura and I dubbed it Bridal Veil Falls, after our favorite waterfall in Yosemite. Jake must have realized it was time to intervene.

"You know, Craig," started Jake, "that leak is a thief. It steals gallons of water from us every day. That costs big bucks over time; plus, it's just a waste!"

It was a brilliant argument. Craig looked at his dog. "You know, you're right. I'll get on it right away," he responded. That very night, Bridal Veil Falls dried up.

For some reason, Jake speaks only when I'm around. No one ever tells me about conversations with the dog that I haven't heard firsthand. His talking has become a perfectly normal part of our lives. When he opens his mouth, we listen and respond as if he's just another human member of the family.

He never really talked to me, though. That is, not until a few weeks ago.

I was working at my computer late one night, with Jake relaxing on his bed near my desk. "Oh, Jake, I'm so tired!" I groaned. He immediately offered advice: "You really need to go upstairs right now and go to bed." Since then he's talked to me about everything from paying bills on time to how to clean the house more efficiently.

Jake

Last week a friend came over for tea. She couldn't decide if she'd prefer green tea or the delectable, vanilla-flavored English Breakfast tea I'd picked up in London. She was leaning toward green tea when, out of the blue and before I could stop him, Jake intervened in his Pooh-ish voice. "You've gotta try the English Breakfast. It's *so* delicious!" (Coincidentally, that was my feeling exactly, but who was I to sway my guest after giving her the choice?)

My friend looked at me askance. "Uh, is something wrong with your throat? You sound kind of sick."

My cheeks got hot. I coughed and cleared my throat. "Yeah, um, something was sort of stuck. I'm okay now." I looked around, and Jake was nowhere to be seen. Then I remembered that he was on a walk with Craig.

I coughed again and changed the subject.

It was a close call. My secret identity had almost been revealed. Through the magic of a child's imagination and a husband's willingness to go along with whatever came out of my/ Jake's mouth, I'd very nearly come to believe my dog could really talk. His way with words proved fun—and useful!—within the family, but perhaps I'd gotten carried away with the effortlessness of being his mouthpiece. It was all coming a bit too naturally. My god, I'd even had conversations with him myself. That should have been warning enough.

I decided I'd have to start keeping a lid on the Lab. After all, we can't have his gift of gab becoming such a habit that he bursts out in conversation in front of just anybody. What would the neighbors think?

So far, so good; Laura recently had some confusion about her homework, and Jake didn't utter a peep. Craig had a choice of going fishing or staying home and helping me with some household projects. Jake's lips were sealed. Craig opted for salmon over sanding.

But our anniversary is next week, and Craig hasn't said a word about it yet. If I bring it up, it would be too cliché. However,

I'm not sure how long Jake is going to be able to hold his tongue. I think he may have to break his silence and have a little talk with Craig soon.

Some things, after all, are worth a little tongue-wagging.

And Babies Made Five
Alyssa Shaffer

When you're trying to start a family, pregnancy becomes one of those things you fantasize about. I had visions of glowing skin, luminous hair, a knowing smile, and a swollen belly that proudly garaged the new life within. I would be strong. I would be active. I would be calm, and nurturing. I would take long walks with Jett, our greyhound, to stay fit and ward off excess pregnancy pounds.

The reality was, I was sick. Not at first, though. In fact, the first trimester of my pregnancy was somewhat of a joke. Since I was carrying twins, my doctors warned me that my chances for morning sickness were exponentially higher than those of someone who had only one life incubating inside her. Expect extreme fatigue, they said—and definitely nausea. My husband, Scott, and I had previously booked a cruise to the Galapagos Islands. Uncertain whether I'd be well enough to weather early pregnancy—yet alone the high seas—we warily went ahead with our travel plans. And the trip proceeded without a hitch. As the boat rocked us to sleep, we lay together in our tiny cabin, dreaming of the new lives waiting to join us and joking about how the lazy sea lions who sunbathed on the shore reminded us of Jett soaking up the rays back home, absorbing the warm sun on his smooth, black fur.

The first clue that this whole pregnancy thing might not be all smooth sailing came shortly after the beginning of my second trimester. I was attempting a Thai chicken curry recipe for dinner one night when I began feeling a little nauseous. The chicken had been thawing all day in the sink, but it seemed innocuous enough when I began slicing it up. Two hours later, I was retching over the toilet—the first of many trips to the bathroom that evening. Jett gave me sympathetic glances and followed my every move. One very long night and dozens of flushes later, I blamed a too-sensitive stomach and cursed myself for not following better food preparation guidelines.

Midway through my fourth month, the pregnancy books that formed a nice stack on the nightstand congratulated me about making it through my first trimester and welcomed me into the glory days of pregnancy—more energy, less fatigue, and a stronger stomach. But it seemed my body hadn't read these books, because about a week after my first attack, I was back in the bathroom and miserable again. This time I ended up in the hospital, frightened and dehydrated from constantly, violently being ill.

It got worse. Much worse. As my pregnancy progressed, so did the incidents of nausea and vomiting. They began to take on a familiar pattern: I'd start to feel nauseous soon after trying to eat, spend the next few hours repeatedly retching, and crawl back into bed, where Jett would curl up beside me, eyeing me with sympathy and concern and nuzzling under my arm. My doctor diagnosed me with *Hyperemesis gravidarum*—a severe form of pregnancy-induced nausea and vomiting. I was admitted to the hospital a handful of times and given IV fluid to prevent dehydration, along with a host of stomach medications designed to keep me from my constant need to throw up. Even a special pump attached to my thigh that administered a constant dose of anti-nausea medication didn't seem to help.

Eventually, even dragging myself to the office seemed a task too great to bear. The process of commuting less than four miles still involved navigating steps and subways, and even getting in and out of the sticky back seat of the taxi overwhelmed me. So by the middle of my seventh month, I gave up trying and put myself on a form of modified bed rest.

Jett was probably the only member of our household happy about this decision. He seemed thrilled that I would no longer be abandoning him each morning in an empty home. Instead, he would have constant—albeit quiet—company to join him throughout his day. Which, I noticed, consisted mostly of sleeping in different areas of the house: on the floor next to the couch in the

Jett

living room; on his oversized leopard-print dog bed in the bedroom; on the rug in front of the air conditioner.

But most of the time, Jett slept curled up next to me on top of our king-size comforter. Shades mostly drawn, pillows plumped around my by-now-ample abdomen, I spent most of my last trimester either tucked into bed or huddled over the toilet. I slept for hours at a time, waking only to force myself to eat something or run to the bathroom. And Jett was there the whole time, concern flashing in his deep brown eyes, following my every movement from bed to bathroom and back again.

The exception came around 4:00 PM, when Jett politely began to request more than just a pat on the head or a cuddle. He needed to go out. I'd usually greet this demand with a groan. Energy levels severely lagging, I dragged myself out of bed and grabbed his leash for our daily half-mile walk in the park.

And it was there that I finally began to remember what it felt like to be a part of the world. Walking with Jett to the dog run in the park or even just around the block brought me back in touch with the rhythms of the neighborhood. I left my clouded state, if only for a half hour or so, and was able to smile at the mothers pushing their strollers, at the doormen who stood guard each afternoon in the same exact place, at the delivery boys rushing to get their goods to their intended destinations as fast as possible. I have Jett to thank for getting me to enjoy the waning days of summer—the late-afternoon sun dipping over the river, an increasingly cool breeze passing through the sidewalks. It reminded me that a world did indeed exist beyond the drawn bedroom shades, and that this phase of my life would soon be coming to an end and I would be able to rejoin that world for good.

On September 13, shortly after I'd taken Jett out on a slightly earlier than usual, abbreviated walk around the block, I took a taxi across town for my regular biweekly obstetrician checkup. I got on the scale in the doctor's office and sighed—I'd gained only five pounds over the course of the pregnancy. I had zero energy and was pale and tired. I was ready for this whole thing to be over. But when my doctor took my blood pressure, she gave me a careful look. "I think you should go to the hospital, just to have them monitor you for a bit," she said. I looked at Scott, surprised. "It's not serious, right?" I asked. "Oh, no, just for observation," she smiled. Scott held my hand, and we walked the ten blocks to the hospital.

Seven hours later, our twins, Nolan and Layla, were born, weighing in at a small—but healthy—three pounds, eleven ounces and three pounds, thirteen ounces, respectively. We found out later that I'd developed a case of preeclampsia, and my doctor was anxious to avoid possible complications from my severely elevated blood pressure. We were not, suffice to say, prepared at that point to have our family nearly double in size. There were dishes left in the sink. The babies' furniture was due to be delivered the next day. And no one had taken Jett out for a proper walk.

Things came together, though, as they tend to do in times of urgency. Our family and friends rallied, packing up necessities for the hospital, sitting in our apartment to await the furniture delivery. A neighbor who also had a greyhound gladly took Jett in for the next week, since Scott was spending most of his spare time either at the hospital with me or sleeping.

Jett was understanding, as always, when Scott did finally come to take him home. And he remained understanding when we brought Nolan home from the hospital, followed a few days later by Layla. He was somewhat confused by these new additions to the household, but I don't think he seriously thought they were there to stay.

Although we swore at the start of the pregnancy that we would not neglect Jett once the babies entered our lives, we inevitably do. It's nearly impossible to give him the same amount of attention he received before. And he puts up with their tugs, pulls, and clumsy explorations of his paws, tail, and coat with about as much patience as anyone could expect.

But at the end of the day, Jett still makes it known that he has unassailable rights in the home. Foremost of these is a good cuddle. Each night he hops onto the bed and curls up next to me, stretching his long limbs out and nuzzling his increasingly gray muzzle beside me. I scratch his ears, which is his cue to roll onto his back and bare his belly. It's his way of telling me that all, indeed, is right in our house once again.

Online Dogging
Melinda J. Combs

I found true love online. Well, I found true doggy
love online.

It all started when I decided to venture into another
relationship after my first canine love, Chief, broke my heart. Our
ten-year bond ended, not from a breakup, but when he passed
away. It took me four months to start thinking about a new
companion, especially because I wanted to honor Chief by giving
myself time between relationships. I didn't want a rebound dog.
I'm not the kind of girl who rushes into another romance quickly.
Besides, I needed enough time to allow my heart to mend as
much as possible.

While walking with my friend Tess along the beach, I
mentioned that it was time to start looking for another dog.

"Looking" was the key word here; I wasn't ready for another commitment, but I wanted to see what kind of dog I could find if I opened my eyes again. Opening my heart, well, that was another matter.

Tess mentioned a website that serves as a clearinghouse for homeless animals waiting to be adopted. She found her cat online, and they've lived happily ever since. So as soon as I got home, I did a brief search, just to "get acquainted with the website," I told myself. Instead of being a woman looking for a man between the ages of thirty-two and thirty-eight and living within ten miles of my zip code, I was now looking for a young, female chocolate Labrador.

When I entered my zip code and hit "go," six dogs popped up onscreen: Dottie in Redondo Beach, Miss Sable Vargas in Chatsworth, Pudding in Ontario, and so on. I viewed their photos, reviewed their personality profiles, and pondered their mixes. Was Pudding my type? Would Miss Sable Vargas and I get along? And then I started to wonder more about what wasn't listed in these dogs' profiles, like if Dottie would chew my shoes, or if Lady Bird liked to play too much.

Because Chief was a yellow Labrador/golden retriever mix, I convinced myself that the next dog after him must be a female chocolate Lab. If I found a girl, I would be less likely to compare her to Chief, and chocolate Labs enchanted me with those irresistible green eyes and big, soft ears. Besides, their renowned playfulness complements my extra energy.

But suddenly, I didn't have the courage to inquire about a dog. I wasn't ready. I couldn't put myself out there, fall in love again, risk another heartbreak. And there wasn't a way to send a wink, a far less risky move than an email or a phone call, to let a dog know about my interest.

I searched the website every few days, fawning and admiring but not ready to make the first move. Simultaneously, Tess emailed me pictures of available dogs she thought I would like. Her messages always read, "Hey, look at this one!" or, "Cute, huh?" One day, I received nine emails from her—talk about working hard to set me up! Of course, my friends and I exchange profiles of men we're interested in. The dialogue is similar, just with a different species.

After too many nights of coming home to an empty house—or often just avoiding coming home altogether—I knew I could not endure the dogless life any more. I was finally ready. My first official inquiry: a chocolate Lab/American Staffordshire terrier mix named Gladys, a puppy who loved to chew and play. In fact, one of her photos showed her happily chewing on a shoe. When I called about her, nervousness struck. Would I say the right thing? What if I sounded like an idiot? When faced with phoning a potential date, I've been known to accidentally identify myself as the guy and ask for me. Would I now call myself Gladys? Fortunately, I didn't. But when I learned more about Gladys and the fact that American Staffordshire terrier is the fancier name for a pit bull, I wasn't sure if she and I would be a match. I hadn't hit it off with a pit bull before. Besides, I wanted a chocolate Lab and didn't want to change types.

A couple days later, I emailed about a purebred chocolate Lab named Madeline. In her photo she was running toward the camera, with big brown eyes and her pink tongue hanging out. When I called about her, again I felt anxious. What if I wasn't good enough for such an official dog, one with papers? Was she out of my league?

The woman from the rescue shelter gently told me I had been beaten to the punch. "Madeline's former owner will be interviewing two potential families this afternoon that want to adopt her, so I'm sure she'll have a new home soon. Madeline's had loads of inquiries."

"I'm happy to hear that she'll be in a new home soon," I told her, disappointed.

That's when I realized it might be a more competitive market than I had originally thought, especially for a female Lab puppy.

In the meantime, I also emailed about a few other dogs, and with some, I didn't get any response. Had they already found someone else? If so, their profiles shouldn't be up anymore, so that those looking for love didn't get their hopes up. I conjured other reasons for such rejection: The rescue organizations were so busy with their work that they just couldn't respond, or they knew the dog and I wouldn't be a good fit, or I sent the email to the wrong address, or their email server crashed. Then I worried that I wasn't as ready as I thought, because if I were ready the dog and I would find each other, and we'd walk off, side by side, into the sunset. Maybe somebody was trying to tell me something and I wasn't listening. Maybe I was obsessing a little.

Still determined to find my chocolate Lab, I looked into some Labrador retriever rescue organizations, and when I emailed about Hershey Kiss, I learned I didn't qualify because I didn't have a back yard. The rejection crushed me. It was time for a self–pep talk: I'm an avid dog-walker, I told myself. There are plenty of dog owners who have yards but don't walk their dogs, ever, and these rescue organizations made a great mistake by not letting me have an available dog. These dogs missed out on something great: me. But I knew plenty of other dogs existed for me. I just needed to keep looking.

I decided to broaden my search, moving beyond my typical

type. After all, don't they say love can be found in the most unexpected places? One evening after spending time online, passing profiles over because the dog was too old, too young, too big, or too small, I stumbled across a rescue shelter's website while looking at a Lab. Once linked to the shelter's pet list, I read every available dog's profile. That's when I found a teddy bear disguised

Marley

as a dog. The profile listed her as an Australian shepherd/clumber spaniel mix, but the notes said, "If you can figure out her breed, please tell us. . . . If there was a breed Clown/Doll, Marley would be it." The three photos showed off her copper body, dappled with white on her chest and toes, her white head, and one copper ear. In one photo, she wore a baseball hat backwards. With her white eyelashes and pink nose, she had me hooked.

I immediately emailed to ask if Marley was still on the market, because I didn't want to get my hopes up only to be disappointed. Within an hour, a reply arrived: "Yes, and she's wonderful." I filled out an application with great trepidation: I had a simultaneous fear of rejection and commitment. Could this be the one? Was I ready? My first application didn't arrive because of computer issues. Maybe the organization thought I was inept at that point. But I tried again, and upon review my application was deemed "flawless." I passed! Somebody liked me, somebody really liked me!

We arranged a meeting at a pet supply store in Santa Monica. In the meantime, Marley's profile circulated among my friends and family, who wanted to see my potential new companion.

Tess said: "Not really your type, but super cute."

My father: "Lots of hair, so shedding may be a problem, but all of your clothes are normally covered in dog hair, so what's the difference?"

My brother: "She needs to go on a diet. She's got pit bull in her too."

And my mother, aware of my tiredness of being alone: "She's adorable."

That Saturday, Tess and I set out on our dog-meeting adventure. First we visited a local animal shelter to look around, just to see if any dog grabbed my attention. I played with a chocolate Lab mix named Sally, but we didn't mesh: Her hyper disposition threw me off balance, and she wouldn't look me in the eye. Moving on, we drove an hour to Santa Monica.

Just in case, I brought a leash.

When I entered the chaotic pet store, Marley walked in behind me, returning from a brief outing with one of the volunteers. Pulling hard on the leash, she wanted back in her crate. I felt a bit disappointed that Marley didn't say hello. But her rescuers greeted me with a hug and a, "We're so glad you're here to meet our girl."

Now it was my turn to take Marley on a walk—to get to know her a little better, so to speak. She lollygagged around the pet store and basically refused to walk too far away, but the minute we turned around, she once again pulled hard on her leash to get back to the store. Apparently, she didn't like being out of her comfort zone, and I wasn't feeling any great connection.

Then I met with Dylan, who had pulled Marley out of the city pound, where she had been "dropped off" a few months before. As a volunteer for the rescue organization, one of Dylan's jobs entails pulling dogs from pounds where they don't have much of a chance. And during one of Dylan's searches she discovered Sasquatch, whom she immediately renamed Marley because her mellowness seemed to parallel Bob Marley's.

While sitting on the grass with Dylan, Tess, and Marley, I studied this overweight, dirty creature. Because her foster mother hadn't had time to bathe her for the big meeting, it forced me to look beyond Marley's appearance and take note of her personality instead. I could get her groomed and on an exercise regime in no time. That's the easy part. It's falling in love that's harder.

Marley sat between us and flopped over on her back so many times I lost count. Her biggest desire? A belly rub. With her pink tongue hanging out constantly (because she has no front teeth), her different colored ears, and her need for affection, she proved hard to resist.

Dylan told us what she knew of Marley's history: an easygoing, low-maintenance dog with a small invisible shield around her, probably from being neglected or left outside for far too long. Marley needed someone who could gently move beyond that shield, someone who could earn her trust, someone who could make her feel more secure. And she said more than once, "She's one of our best dogs. She's a bit of a nut because she'll try to jump up on a car or something high, but she's great. If I could take her, I would, but I already have four dogs."

Before I could fully commit, though, I wanted Marley to look me in the eyes. After a few minutes of watching her intently, she made eye contact. Because Tess knew that mattered to me, she immediately enthused, "She did it! She's looking at you! See? This could be the one!"

I didn't feel an instant spark with Marley, but I agreed to love her anyway because I knew I could provide her with a good home, and I wanted to give her a chance—to give us a chance. Because they still needed to do a home inspection, Marley couldn't come home with me that day. I had to wait even longer. But when I said, "Goodbye, I'll see you in a few days" with my hand hanging onto the crate, Marley reached her paw up to touch my hand. That moment melted away my concerns. Maybe we'd be okay after all.

Now that Marley and I have been together for almost four months, I often laugh about my path to finding her. The first time I visited a shelter in search of a new companion, a volunteer told me, "Have faith. The dog will find you. It may take time."

Isn't that just like true love?

Sage the Hollywood Dog

Julia Fulton

The nomadic lifestyle of a struggling actress in Hollywood kept me throwing both possessions and relationships overboard. Plants and men didn't survive long. The only constants in my life were my two dogs, Sage and Cyrano.

Two weeks into our first January in a new apartment, a 6.8 earthquake hit Los Angeles at 4:17 in the morning. We were sitting on a fault line directly south of the quake's epicenter in Northridge, just over the Sepulveda Pass in the Valley. Normally I would have been snoring along with Cyrano, my young golden retriever. But in this predawn darkness I was tying on my sneakers. Sage, my nine-year-old Beardy mix, had been up for half an hour or so. He whined and nudged me until I dressed. It was odd for him; maybe he didn't feel well. Then it hit.

The first jolt rocked us up and down; it sounded like a freight train was derailing underneath the bedroom. My bedstand fell over, along with the glasses I needed to see with; bookcases toppled, plants upended, and the kitchen cabinets spilled their contents, soaking broken china and glass in soy sauce, olive oil, and spice bottles. We stumbled and fell, scrambling for the living room. All light from the neighborhood was extinguished. Sage headed for the front door, his blond coat glowing from some invisible source. *Good boy,* I thought. He was herding us to the doorframe, a little tip the earthquake experts always give you. Sage licked Cyrano's ears and nuzzled my neck. He smelled like clean cotton socks. When the awful roaring stopped, there wasn't a sound from the street. The slow ebb and flow of the aftershocks continued in silence, like waves lapping under a shipwreck. This was not the first bind we had gotten into, Sage and me. The first day I met him he had saved me, in fact.

My family home on the Jersey Shore always had a dog, cat, ferret, hamsters, mice, and guinea pigs. But now that I was living alone in Los Angeles, any space seemed empty without that kind of life breathing around me. So the first thing I did when I got a house was look for a dog. The West Valley pound was a depressing cinder block surrounded by high fences and topped with barbed wire. The pound's attendant pointed at the narrow corridors.

"The ones with the red ribbons on the cage are out of time!" she shouted. I passed the cells, the dogs pawing the mesh, all of them like versions of the same universal mutt, black and thin: part Doberman, rottweiler, Lab? This was not a good idea; there were no baskets of puppies anywhere.

I stopped in front of a cell that seemed to contain a large black bear. We locked eyes and he lunged for me, teeth bared, snarling with rage at the wire fence separating us. He stood up and the fence swayed against his weight. His teeth snapped against the mesh. Suddenly, a yellow dog sidled up to the bear and gently grabbed the flap of fur under his dribbling mouth. The bear stood down from the fence and sat back. The yellow dog led the bear to the back of the cell near the water bowl, then padded back to me, grinning, and pushed one paw through a gap in the wire. I sat down on the wet concrete and stroked him. We looked at each other. He was filthy, his ribs visible under the matted coat. But his head, his magnificent head! Part collie, part shepherd, but mostly he looked like the Disney dog in the movies. His large eyes were a peculiar golden yellow, ringed with dramatic black like exotic mascara. His ears were shaggy; his tail was long and plumed. His smile showed white, aristocratic teeth. *A gentleman fallen on hard times,* I thought. *A prince disguised as a pauper.*

I waited the requisite two-week period to see if an owner

showed up to claim him, worried that he would disappear just as magically as he had appeared, that I would never get to hold him and give him back his title. On the fifteenth day I was at the door of the pound before it opened. But I wasn't alone. There were five other people there: a mother and daughter holding an expensive collar and leash, a young guy stepping down from a truck, and

Sage

a confident couple holding hands. We knew we had come for the same dog, the one who did the magic trick with the bear, who shook hands and winked through the cell. There was a bidding war. We were fighting about a sick mutt from the pound. Checkbooks were out.

But this was my mate, my answer to the ache and loneliness that consumed my days, my reward for the endless rounds of auditions. I tallied up what I had in the bank. The truck driver folded when we reached the hundred-dollar mark. The yuppie couple gave up when we hit $250. The daughter started crying. "Four hundred dollars," I said, cold as ice. Her mother gave a sharp grunt and they headed for the door. The employees shook my hand, delighted at the charitable contribution. "He's a wheaten terrier mix," said one, "My grandmother has two of them."

"Actually, he's mostly bearded collie," said another. "He's a herding dog. Smart, independent."

"Well, otterhounds are rare," said a third. "But he really has the line, the color, the nose."

Wheaten terrier, bearded collie, otterhound, whatever. He trotted out the door at my side, his head high, his golden eyes snapping with pleasure. He jumped into the front seat of my blue Mustang convertible as calmly as if he'd sat there all his life.

The first thing he did when we got to my house was walk across water. Literally. He mistook the blue pool cover for some sort of carpet and just stepped onto it, heading for the back door. Before I could shout a warning, his feet had started to sink. He just kept moving, trotting so lightly over the pool that he got to the other side with his toes barely damp. He glanced back at me and smiled. I called him Sage because he was wise, but I gave it the French pronunciation (rhymes with "Taj").

The vet said he was probably seven months old. Riddled with fleas and worms and ticks, and about twenty-five pounds underweight, he was too weak to walk more than a block or two at first. Soon he was filling out and growing a coat that would be thick and long, the tips of his floppy ears dipped in the same black ink that rimmed his eyes. He had a quick knack for climbing trees after squirrels.

We were inseparable until I got a job in a play called, strangely enough, *Dog Logic*. When I got back from my first day, the den window facing the street was shattered, glass all over the yard. I was stunned. Where had he run? The street was a busy thoroughfare to the freeways; he wouldn't stand a chance. The den window looked worse from the inside, and there was blood on the sill. I found him lying under my desk, rueful and wounded. Sage trusted me, knew that I would come back. I promised him I always would. It's one of the few promises I have ever kept.

As he grew and gained weight, he became a prankster; there was a gaiety and slyness in him that would evaporate my angst and feed my soul. He had a little orange ball that he squeezed for squeaky songs. Harpo Marx had his horn to speak for him, and Sage had this orange ball. Soon I had collected a pack of small stuffed animals for him—rabbits and raccoons, beavers and bobcats. They all spoke when you squeezed their middles. Sage was overjoyed. Finally, he had a pack that could speak for him! He dropped his orange ball into the communal basket and tenderly tucked his new brood around him.

¡Hasta la vista! he'd growl to my mother as she left for the bathroom. Bouncing into the dinner party, he'd shout, *Hello, my friends! My name is Henri! Would you like to go fishing with me?* Sleepy mornings he'd sidle up to my bed and whisper, *I am Fabian the*

Fox. Would you like a café au lait? Watching the evening news, he'd push Punk the Skunk against the TV set. *What's that smell?* he'd say, squeezing. *What's that* smell? But the baby wolf remained his favorite. The company who made the animals even honored their promise to replace any animal that stopped speaking. I'm sure they didn't anticipate that actually happening. But when the toy no longer responded to Sage's squeezes, he became worried, frantic.

The replacement arrived within the week, to his immense relief. "Dear Julia," the note included in the box said, "We are very sorry that Wilhelmina stopped speaking. Here is your new baby wolf." We took a little advantage of their service, replacing Bennie the Beaver and Fabian the Fox before they finally caught us with the rabbit, Henri. They sent a new one, with a note that reprimanded us: "Henri was very dirty and missing an eye. We do not think you are taking good care of him." Oh, but Sage *was*; he was just squeezing them mute.

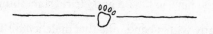

I was doing a recurring role on a soap opera when one day on the set I noticed a dog that could have been Sage's cosmic cousin. His trainer, Mathilde, worked for Universal Studios and had gotten Freddie from a pound about seventy-five miles south of where I met Sage. Freddie was playing Einstein in the *Back to the Future*

movies, and the studio wanted an insurance double. Sage spent some afternoons learning camera sign language at Universal. He was so quick, so nonchalant about it that the studio asked to name my price. *Name my price.* Hmm. *A house in Provence?* But no, Sage was not for sale. He did do a few scenes in the movies, though, and I pocketed a modest retainer fee for collars, dog treats, and trips across the States.

One spring morning Sage and I found ourselves standing in a long line outside Sunset-Gower Studios. We were number 173 in a crowd that swelled to four hundred by noon. The Chuck Wagon dog food empire was doing a national search for the "new Chuck Wagon dog," and every canine in Hollywood wanted the job. The closer we got to the entrance, the friendlier the other combatants became. Stories were shared; rumors began.

"I hear they put you through these tests," said one heavy woman with a shuddering spaniel.

"I hear you have to have a good trick, something unusual," said another guy with a bandanna that matched his Labrador retriever's.

"My dog can get a beer out of the refrigerator," said one tattooed young thug as his rottweiler glared around the lot.

One inconspicuous fellow whispered to me, "If looks win, your guy scores."

We were admitted in a group of five. There were massive wagon wheels and bales of hay on a brightly lit stage. Barely visible cameras surrounded us, and the judges were faceless shadows against the wall. I was sweating; Sage didn't bark on command, or wave, or roll over. I knew he wouldn't touch a bowl of Chuck Wagon dog food. I glanced at the rottweiler. I hoped they didn't have any beers backstage.

There was a surprise test after all: Each dog had to chase a miniature chuck wagon around the bales of hay, without barking or attacking it. No one was very good at that. Our turn came, and I unleashed Sage. He immediately trotted to stage left and sat down. The camera operator gasped: "That dog just sat down on the mark! He hit the mark!"

Some actors have trouble hitting the tiny cross of masking tape that directs you to the camera's view, but Sage didn't even look down. Then he sat up when I asked him to and almost waved. He cocked his head, his shaggy ears alert. He winked at the judges. The little wagon started buzzing behind the bale of hay. It toured around the stage, directed by remote control, and for a moment Sage was still, his head tipped to one side. There was no sound, no breath from anyone. I could hear the film whirring in the camera. Then Sage leapt gracefully towards the wagon and trotted alongside it, friendly and grinning. We got the job.

He was an instant celebrity. Papers interviewed us, and news channels taped Sage climbing trees and shaking hands; he was the perfect "rags to riches" story. His Chuck Wagon ads were circulated in most national papers for two years, which was more exposure than I was getting guest-starring on episodic television. Sage's confidence and humor helped me to weather the arrogant producers, casting directors, and agents.

We moved again; we were always moving. Television money allowed me to get a small, pretty house in Woodland Hills. The six-foot-high hedges that surrounded the yard were no match for Sage's leaping capacity, and I heard my new neighbors calling out, almost daily, "That yellow dog is in the yard again!" Turned out he was crazy about the young couple's retriever, a blond bombshell named Chessie. Their daily trysts introduced me to my new best friends next door. Even when we moved back over the hill to West Hollywood, the friendship continued.

When Chessie had a litter (sired by another retriever), we adopted the surprise runt that wouldn't sell. He was a tiny wrinkled raisin of a dog. But his nose was as big as he was, so I named him Cyrano after the great romantic de Bergerac. He was seven weeks old when we took him home, and he promptly came down with parvovirus, almost always fatal to puppies. One of his eyes turned blue and opaque with the sickness. Sage and I sat together by his little pillow, where Cyrano panted through the fever. But he was a tough little raisin with a big nose, and he pulled through and grew into a goofy pacifist, a real *doggy* dog. He taught Sage how to roll in the grass, how to enjoy his food, how to turn his nose into the wind.

Cyrano had a talent, too: He could find a tennis ball anywhere—a bush, a gutter, the middle of the desert. We had baskets of balls that Cyrano would sniff like a connoisseur, picking out just the right one to settle with by the couch. Each ball held a Proustian memory for him; each ball was unique. It baffled Sage, who would just look at me as if to say, *Can you believe this guy?* The first time Sage saw Cyrano roll in the mud, he was shocked. Sage wanted dirt and sand immediately brushed out of his coat. He sidestepped puddles and refused to walk in the rain. A British director once remarked to me, "Sage is a jacket-and-tie sort of dog, isn't he? And Cyrano is more ROTC."

Years passed. Sage was thirteen when I met a man Sage finally approved of and married him. Allan and Sage were immediate comrades; I'd enter the room and they would both look at me in a way that embarrassed me.

Allan already had a cat, Zoey, and she had never come close to a dog. She was skittish for weeks, and then one night tiptoed up to a dozing Sage and touched his nose with hers. Sage woke and smiled at her, and she quickly moonwalked back out of the room. But the ice had been broken, and Zoey became enamored of him. She left a dead rat in his food bowl one day, scaring the hell out of both dogs. Then she tried leaving live game on the stairs, in his bed: bewildered mice and squirrels and doves, even a hummingbird. But when her hunting failed to charm Sage, she stopped. She began to copy canine behavior, taking walks and naps with the boys. Cyrano she teased like a kid brother: She'd hide under our bed until Cyrano lay down nearby. Then Zoey would dart a paw out, bopping him. But the joke grew old, and she started stroking him instead. Cyrano loved her. He loved everybody, especially the toddlers he'd see on our walks. His tail would swish madly; he wanted a baby.

Finally our pack swelled with our baby girl. We gathered every night in our den, the baby at my breast, Allan reading, Cyrano snoring, and Sage nuzzling my palm with soft, hot breath. His amber eyes glowing, he would study my face, making sure I grasped how wonderful this was.

The baby had her first steps and her first birthday, and the fall deepened into the early twilights and soft chill of California's winter. Sage had made almost eighteen years of journeys with me, but he was thinking about making his final one alone. Christmas was coming, but Sage was fading. His coat had whitened, had lightened into a silken cloak, a wizard's cape. He was serene, but I often caught him staring at me with a strange, distant expression. The weeks were warm and sunny, and we cuddled together in the yard often. I brushed him and massaged his stiff limbs. Our girl toddled in the grass, holding my hand. My other palm rested flat on Sage's narrow back as we circled the ficus tree in our backyard. It was one of his last walks outside. He was falling a lot, his frame shrinking, his coat luminous, transparent. Resting in his bed, he squeezed his baby wolf. *Think only good thoughts,* he said.

It was the morning of Christmas Eve. Our small evergreen scented the house. I lit candles by Sage's bed and waved a fragrant bundle of sage over his head. Some ritual was called for. It was time.

At the vet, he smiles at us as he lies on the table. I whisper to him about the beach we are running on. The sand is white and soft, and the sunset fierce yellow. There is a ship coming across the lavender waves, and Sage sees it. He is running now, running along the shore. His head is up, smelling the wind, trembling, not acquiescing but not resisting, either. He is moments from leaving. Sage closes his magnificent golden eyes and rests. I take off his bright green collar and release him from service. My lips kiss the top of his silken head. He smells like clean cotton socks.

His ashes sit in a red cedar box that our little girl, Simone, got hold of yesterday. I am pregnant with a boy, a surprise, a miracle. Sage must have seen this little fellow on his way up and given him a nudge. I reach out for Simone, but she is smitten with the box. She pushes it along the floor; she puts one of her blankets on top of it. "Shush shush," she is saying to the box. "Night night."

Firstborn

Lisa Vollmer

Three years ago, my relationships with some of my closest girlfriends started to change forever. The changes were sudden and dramatic, predictable and yet somehow still surprising—understandable on a rational level, but entirely unacceptable on an emotional one.

It all started when I innocently opened an email from my close friend Laura, who insisted that we needed to chat on the phone as soon as possible. "Much to catch up on," she wrote. The subtle urgency in her message caught my attention. Instinctively, I knew that "much to catch up on" meant only one thing: Laura was pregnant.

My instincts proved right. When Laura finally told me the big news after a few minutes of small talk, I was able to eke out a sufficiently convincing high-pitched congratulatory squeal—the one that girlfriends expect from each other when they announce the truly momentous developments in their lives. Unsure of the proper protocol beyond "congratulations," I asked the obvious question.

"Did you guys . . . plan this?" I asked tentatively (even though the words that had actually popped into my head were "Did you do this to yourself . . . on *purpose?*"). As it turned out, she and her husband *had* planned it, and they could not have been happier. They were about to become parents for the first time.

In the three years since Laura's announcement, it seems as though dozens of other friends have called or written with the same news. And every time a friend tells me she's expecting, the same sequence of events ensues: my high-pitched congratulatory squeal, her filling me in (unprompted) on the details of how she and her husband conceived, and a comprehensive summary of her pregnancy to date. Six months later, I'm treated to the birth story, which inevitably involves the words "dilated," "membrane," "mucus plug," and other terms that make me squeamish and uncomfortable. From that point on, our telephone conversations, which used to end with "I'll meet you on Friday—we'll grab lunch," now end with "I have to go for now—Timmy is projectile-vomiting."

It's not that I'm not happy for my friends; I am. I just can't relate to their enthusiasm, since I was born without maternal instincts. I've never longed for a baby, or even been able to imagine myself with one for more than five minutes. I suspect that I'm actually allergic to children in the same way that some people are violently allergic to cats: Even being in the same room with one is getting way too close, and having one of your own is entirely out of the question.

It doesn't help that I seem to have some sort of powerful magnetic chip embedded in my neck that ensures that every time I board an airplane, I'm always seated next to the one screaming toddler on board. But it's not just the screaming. There are the temper tantrums in public places, the endless stream of bodily fluids spewing from every imaginable orifice, the squirming and crawling and climbing in restaurant booths, department stores, and airplane seats. There's the trail of sticky purple juice and Cheerios that seems to follow them wherever they go, the way every sound they emit is high pitched, the way they defiantly refuse to take naps or eat vegetables. There's the way they always seem to be getting into something that they shouldn't, making messes where none existed before. Yes, when it comes down to it, children make me incredibly uneasy.

It could be that I'm a horrible person for feeling this way. Maybe the same gene that was supposed to supply my maternal instincts got left behind in the womb somewhere (along with the one that was supposed to provide me with Heidi Klum's metabolism). Or maybe I've just seen too many moms looking exhausted and defeated as they grocery shop, pretending not to notice their little hooligans squealing and screeching, gleefully pulling cereal boxes off shelves as they careen down the aisles. Whatever the reason, I find myself approaching thirty, the daylight saving time of my life, and my biological clock has steadfastly refused to "spring ahead." Sometimes I think it's in an entirely different time zone altogether.

Even though I've never wanted children, the urge to nurture and protect someone who needs me desperately is not an entirely unfamiliar notion. In my early- to mid-twenties, I ached for a dog the way some women my age ached for a baby. Some of my female friends would feel pangs of maternal longing when they'd see a baby in a shopping mall—I'd feel pangs of maternal longing when I'd see a corgi in Central Park. I had grown up with dogs, but four years of college followed by two years in a tiny Manhattan apartment followed by two years living overseas meant that the timing had never been quite right. My husband, Brian—along with the rest of my family—tried to appease me with corgi-related gifts: corgi greeting cards, corgi stuffed toys, corgi calendars, corgi books. But I still wanted the real thing.

The real thing came into my life two and a half years ago in the form of a three-year-old Pembroke Welsh Corgi named Arby. Arby was my consolation prize for tolerating an unplanned pit stop in my husband's career—a pit stop that would move us from London to Dallas for a yearlong job rotation. By asking me to move to Dallas, Brian was asking me to give up my job and my friends and move to an unfamiliar city where I wouldn't know a soul. If my sanity—and therefore our marriage—was going to survive the move, Brian and I were either going to get a dog or live in different cities for twelve months. We both chose the dog.

But while I was in England, preparing to move from a glamorous European capital to the setting for the cheesiest prime-time soap of the 1980s, my future dog was dealing with problems of his own half a world away. One May afternoon, a motorist spotted Arby lying in a ditch on the side of a road near Little Rock, Arkansas. The kind driver pulled over, scooped Arby into her back seat, took him home, and tried for weeks to find his owners. When no one claimed him, she called the closest rescue group and asked if they could help find him a new home.

I spotted Arby's photo on the Internet a few weeks later, along with the story of how he had been found. As it turned out,

Arby hadn't been starving on the streets of Arkansas: he weighed fifty-three pounds when the rescue group took him in—a full twenty pounds above the average weight for a male corgi. "Arby is HUGE," said the description next to his picture. The liberal

Arby

use of capital letters conveyed the gravity of the situation. "Because he is EXTREMELY food oriented, Arby would do best with an owner who understands that corgis will do ANYTHING for food and must be handled appropriately in this regard." And then the ad threw in a little bit of tough love: "He is looking for a family that will love him enough to say NO when those big brown eyes beg for treats."

I knew right away that Brian and I were meant to give Arby a home. After all, we were also extremely food oriented (under the right circumstances we, too, would do anything for food). And when I read that he would prefer a home where he'd be the only dog, as he "seemed to like people better than other dogs," I knew with even greater certainty that we were a perfect match: In general, I liked dogs better than other people.

A few weeks later, we met Arby's foster parents, who would ultimately decide whether we were a suitable family for him. "He's not the type of dog that's going to run to the front door and jump on you as soon as you walk in the door," warned Beth, Arby's foster mom. And it seemed she was right—Arby didn't really pay much attention to Brian and me the first time we met him.

We couldn't take our eyes off of *him*, though. He was a classic Pem—very long and low to the ground, with short legs that seemed out of proportion with his substantial heft. In his online adoption ad, Beth had described him as a "linebacker of a corgi," referring to the extra twenty pounds he carried. But like a linebacker, he also appeared not to have a neck. His foxlike head seemed to be attached directly to his kielbasa sausage–like body, with nothing visibly connecting the two.

He was the most handsome dog I had ever seen.

"Does he fetch?" I asked Bob, Beth's husband.

"I don't know. But we can find out," Bob said, reaching for a tennis ball. He threw it across the living room. Arby followed the arc of the ball with his eyes, then watched where it landed. He looked at the ball, then looked back at Bob, as if to say, *You know, you dropped something there.*

But it didn't matter whether he was aloof. Or overweight. Or that he wouldn't play fetch. We loved him anyway, and we told Beth and Bob that we wanted to take him home.

Within a few weeks, we did take him home, and it turned

out to be the most important thing that we had done since we'd gotten married two years before. It was an especially momentous occasion for me: The fact that Arby and I had found each other was the stuff children's books were made of. I thought of him as my Velveteen Corgi: I loved him so much that one day he became real.

I wanted to tell everyone about him: family, friends . . . anyone whose contact information I had ever obtained. *But does anyone actually do that?* I wondered. I had certainly been on the receiving end of dozens of joyous emails, photos, and stories sent by proud new parents. So it seemed only appropriate to share my happy news with the people closest to me, even if the object of my maternal affection didn't happen to be human. Inspired by the countless exuberant emails that I had received over the past few years, I started drafting my own announcement in my head:

Sunday, 19 July 2003
Subject: Welcome to our Family, Arby Vollmer

Dear friends and family,
    On July 18, 2003 at 8:05 PM, Brian and I welcomed Arby Vollmer into our family. Arby arrived at our home perfectly healthy (with the exception of some loose stools and bad breath), measuring twenty-nine inches long and

weighing in at a whopping forty-five pounds. Everything about him is simply perfect—right down to his ten tiny toes and, well, his *other* ten tiny toes. Delivery went smoothly, although Mom and Dad encountered some difficulty picking him up and putting him into the car, as he is approximately twenty pounds overweight and does not have sufficiently long legs to jump into the back seat on his own. But Mom and Dad only had to push for a minute or two, and then it was over! Arby was in our house a mere twenty minutes later.

Mom, Dad, and pooch are all settling in at home and are doing well; Mom is getting used to the early morning feedings, while Dad is getting accustomed to the midnight potty breaks. We can't say we weren't warned about the lack of sleep!

Thanks to all who offered their support and prayers during this exciting time for our family. We just can't wait for you to meet Arby in person! In the meantime, here are sixty-two pictures so that you, too, can fawn over our little sweet pea.

Love,

Lisa, Brian, and Arby Vollmer

My enthusiasm over Arby only intensified as the months went on. I took him with me whenever I could, and I'd watch people turn around, stare at him, and smile wherever we went; I suddenly understood what it must feel like to be extraordinarily attractive. My husband and I took pictures of him obsessively, the way all new parents take photos of their newborns. I thought everything he did was adorable: the way he slept on his back with all four legs in the air, the way he ran to the window and wiggled his little bunny tail if you told him there was a squirrel outside. I wanted everyone I knew—everyone I had *ever* known—to understand just how precious he was, and how happy I was to have found him.

I wanted to compile all of the pictures into an online slide show, which would include Brian, Arby, and me in every possible permutation imaginable: Arby and Mom. Arby and Dad. Arby and Mom and Dad. Arby by himself. Arby and Mom in the living room. Arby and Dad in the living room. Arby and Mom and Dad in the living room. . . . Some of the photos would include clever captions in quotation marks, intended to capture what Arby would be saying at that very moment if he could talk. Underneath the photo of Arby with another dog at the dog park, the caption would read, "You can sniff mine if I can sniff yours." Accompanying the photo of Arby rolling around in the grass? A caption that read, "They won't know I've rolled in poop until *after* we get home!"

Of course, there would be photos documenting every milestone in Arby's life, too (and as a new parent, I could define "milestone" as liberally as I wanted): Arby's First Trip to the Dog Park. Arby's First Day at the Beach. Arby Goes to Wine Country. Arby Gets a Bath. The list could go on.

And then there were the Christmas cards. Every year, our mailbox was inundated with Christmas cards, some from people we barely knew—and a few from people I was certain we'd never met—that had glossy photos of children on the front. (Forget about peace on Earth, goodwill toward men, I'd concluded; the holidays are a rare opportunity to brag about your children in a socially acceptable way.) It didn't seem fair that I would be left out of the merriment simply because my "child" had four legs instead of two. I could dress up Arby in some sort of humiliating holiday outfit ("Arby the Red-Nosed Corgi," perhaps?) and photograph him in front of an entirely contrived holiday tableau.

But then I remembered a card we'd received the previous year. It was from a wealthy executive who worked at Brian's company. I had never met this man, let alone his offspring, but he and his wife still sent us a Christmas card with a black-and-white photo of their five children on the front. They were all dressed in pressed khaki and crisp white linen, running hand in hand on a sandy beach towards the camera. Inside, the card read "Laugh. Love. Celebrate. Rejoice. The Johnsons, 2003."

I decided that it would be fun to send out a similarly pretentious card to friends, family, and a random selection of people that I had never met. There would be a photo of Arby emblazoned on the front of each one. We'd get a dramatic shot of him running down a beach, legs stretched out in front of him, paw prints visible in the sand behind him, ears flattened against his head, a stick dangling from his mouth. The greeting inside would read, "Run. Fetch. Eat. Poop. The Vollmers, 2004."

Of course, no personalized Christmas card would be complete without one of those holiday "newsletters"—the kind I had eschewed for so many years, with their reckless abuse of the exclamation point and self-indulgent use of the third-person perspective:

December, 2004

Dear Friends and Family,

Holiday greetings from the Vollmers!! This past year has been a very exciting one for the Vollmers. Brian got a promotion at work and is now the senior vice president of investment research at his firm. Lisa wrote three books this year, and she has also written numerous articles that have appeared in national magazines.

But of course, Lisa and Brian's single greatest achievement this year has been adopting their four-year-old dog, Arby. He is an absolute joy, and Lisa and Brian feel very blessed to have found such an extraordinary canine! Just last month, Arby finished first in his weekly obedience class and has learned "sit," "down," and "give me a kiss" in just a few short weeks. Arby has also been honing his herding skills at the local off-leash park, where he confidently chases dogs twice his size around in circles. With all the exercise and sensible eating, he has lost eight pounds in the last few months (and remember—that's fifty-six pounds to him!), so he is very close to reaching his goal weight of forty pounds. He has never felt better! When he's not hard at work, he enjoys going for walks, riding in the car with all of the windows rolled down, chasing neighborhood cats, and convincing Mom and Dad to feed him more than they should. But more than anything, Arby enjoys spending time with his new family.

Lisa and Brian wish you and yours a very joyous
and memorable holiday season—may 2005 bring you
nothing but health, happiness, and lots of belly rubs!!

Hugs and slobbery kisses,
Lisa, Brian, and Arby Vollmer

Whether I could capture it in an email, bringing Arby into our
house turned out to be a lot more like having a baby than I had
anticipated. My correspondence with his "foster mom" in the
weeks leading up to his adoption should have provided my
first clue. I had written to Beth to ask for a list of things I would
need to pick up before Arby arrived. The first item on the list—
ironically—was a box of baby wipes. "I know, yuck!" Beth wrote.
"But sometimes he needs his bottom wiped, and this is the most
expedient way of doing it—sometimes he can get 'stuff' stuck up
under his nubby little tail, and he will need freshening." The next
item on the list was a package of eye wipes. "Arby's left eye tends
to get a bit goopy in the morning," Beth explained.

"Stuff"? "Freshening"? "Goop"? All of a sudden, I worried
that maybe I wasn't ready for this.

And I soon learned that there would be more than just stuff
and goop involved; there would also be lots of poop, drool, and—

perhaps most pernicious of all—dog hair. Balls of it float across my hardwood floors like tumbleweed on a prairie, and the stuff embeds itself stubbornly in the fibers of our rugs and carpets. I still don't understand how such a relatively compact dog can produce such volumes of hair, but the evidence is everywhere, no matter how frequently I run the vacuum. Arby is a tricolor corgi, too; somehow his black hair ends up on our white carpets, his white hair ends up on our dark clothing, and his brown hair seems to end up everywhere else, including, on occasion, our dinner plates.

Arby can make a mess in less innocent ways, too. More than once, I've come home to find damp bits of cardboard scattered across my dining room floor—the remains of disemboweled dog-biscuit boxes, whose entire contents have been emptied and devoured in my absence. Once I found a trail of plastic from individually wrapped doggie chews that had been purchased in a ninety-count box; by counting the wrappers, I figured out that Arby had scarfed down at least nine of them while I was gone. I've spent Saturday nights cleaning green-tinged dog puke from my garage floor after transgressions like these. I've even come home to a house filled with smoke from Arby's unsuccessful attempt to nab a rotisserie chicken that we'd left sitting on our stovetop after dinner. (He didn't reach the chicken, but he reached the knob that controlled the burner, promptly setting the chicken—and the plate on which it sat—on fire). The fire department came to our rescue, with their pick axes, flame-retardant suits, and hoses in tow. Even after the flames had been extinguished, my house smelled of charred poultry for days.

There aren't just messes to deal with, though. There are the sleepless nights that are an inevitable part of parenthood. I've crawled out of bed in the middle of the night to the barely audible sound of Arby whimpering apologetically, letting me know that he just can't hold it until morning. We've stayed up with him through a few mysterious illnesses, debating whether to take him to the emergency vet clinic at three in the morning. We've spent thousands of dollars at the vet's office so they can remove troublesome lumps and bumps, take x-rays to determine whether he's swallowed something nefarious, and surgically remove burrs from his inner ear. And we've never thought twice about the inconvenience or the expense of it all. It suddenly dawned on me: Were we becoming bona fide parents without even knowing it? Was I all of a sudden . . . *maternal?*

It was entirely possible that Arby had awakened something maternal within me—even if it was only a slightly better understanding of what it meant to be a mother. For the longest time, I couldn't relate to the tears that moms describe when they drop their children off at school on the first day of kindergarten—I would have thought that they'd throw elaborate parties to celebrate the few hours of peace they'd now be able to enjoy. It was only after I had to leave Arby with the dog sitter for the first time that I felt the pangs of separation anxiety—at once irrational and totally overwhelming.

Before Arby, I didn't understand how parents could act so selflessly without complaining—how they could put up with so few hours of uninterrupted sleep, the stains on the furniture, the thousands of diaper changes, and the myriad other inconveniences that come with putting someone else's needs before your own. Arby taught me that it was possible—even for me. I surprised myself with the depth of my affection for my little companion; I really *could* make sacrifices for his well-being without the slightest hint of regret or resentment. And having a dog—like having a baby—requires plenty of sacrifice: leaving dinner parties early to go home and let the dog out, giving up spontaneous weekend trips because we can't find a sitter, skipping the gym because Arby desperately wants to go for a walk. But no matter how inconvenient it can sometimes be, I've never once questioned whether it's worth it.

I'm endlessly fascinated by his range of expressions: His tiny dog eyebrows can instantly transform his face from quizzical to concerned to indifferent to annoyed. I'm continually impressed by his corgi build and stature, the way he manages to look both regal and comical at the same time. And no matter how many times I take him for a walk, I still giggle when I watch his little bunny-like tail move back and forth while his ears flop up and down to the same metronomic rhythm of his jog. I laugh when I watch him run around an off-leash dog park, persistently herding dogs twice his size and speeding around in circles. And every time I'm alone in my house overnight, I am grateful that Arby's ears and his bark are the biggest things about him.

I'm always amused by the way his head tilts to one side when I ask him a question, because I can tell that he really *wants* to understand what I'm saying. And when I have trouble sleeping (which is more often than not), I find instant relaxation when I peer over the side of the bed and see Arby sprawled languidly on his side, his short legs stretched in front of him. I take comfort in his repertoire of little noises, too: the sound of him lapping up water from his bowl, licking his chops while he's napping (presumably because he's dreaming about his next meal), the gentle *click clack* of his tiny toenails against the hardwood floors of our house.

Some people love dogs because they provide acceptance and unconditional love. Indeed, Arby makes me feel as though I'm the most wonderful person in the universe—at least in his admittedly limited universe. But I don't just love him because he wags his tail and jumps up to greet me every time I walk in the front door; I love him because he reminds me that the things that we want most in our lives can actually exceed our expectations. When I think of all of the things I've longed for in my life—whether it's a job, a vacation, a car, a house, a boyfriend—the sense of exhilaration that comes with finally attaining them has eventually faded, giving way to the inevitable realization that things never quite make us as happy as we predicted they would. For me, Arby has been the foot-tall exception to this pattern. I'm just as enamored of him today as I was the day I brought him home two years ago. As silly as it may sound to those who don't consider themselves "dog people," he reminds me daily that you *can* eventually get what you wish for—and that (unlike so many other things) getting what you want can actually bring you more happiness than you ever thought possible.

Okay, I admit it: Maybe I'm more obsessed with my dog than I should be. If my neighbors ever heard me singing to him at the top of my lungs, replacing the word "baby" with the word "Arby" in whatever song happens to be playing, they'd surely think I was crazy. And that's fine. Because by singing ridiculous songs to my dog, I'm reminded of what it's like to be a kid again—how liberating it is to be thoroughly silly, to sing, and to love, for that matter, without the slightest trace of self-consciousness. And even though he's not a human being, he is—for now, at least—my baby.

Is it exactly the same thing as having a "real" baby? Of course not. For one thing, a dog can't take care of you when you get old (of course, he can't scream *"Mommy!"* at the top of his lungs in a public place, either, which brings its own kind of fulfillment). And you can't push dogs to achieve things in their lives that you couldn't quite attain during your own, which is—let's face it—one of the reasons people have kids in the first place.

But even if having a dog isn't exactly the same as having a child, it's the best I can do when it comes to being maternal—at least for now. Like any child—human or canine—Arby gets into things he shouldn't, makes messes where none existed before, regularly wakes me up in the middle of the night, and spews an endless stream of bodily fluids out of every orifice. But I've come to learn that none of that really matters—I still love him anyway.

Maybe there's hope for me after all.

The Point
of No Return

Tracy Teare

The day my dog, Maggie, snapped at my two-year-old
daughter, I knew we'd reached the point of no return. A
dog bite is nothing to take lightly, but because the recipient was
my daughter, and because this was one event of many in the past
five years, it was clear that we had to take action.

Any dog adopted from a shelter is bound to bring along a
certain amount of quirks, and Maggie certainly had her fair share.
My husband, Matt, and I fell for her at once, though she kept to the
back of her kennel and looked scared to death. The size of a small
Lab, Maggie was completely black, with the pointy ears and tail
of a German shepherd. When we signed the papers and brought
her home, she was skittish and anxious. In our great excitement to
have a dog at last, my husband and I took her directly to nearby

conservation land for some time off the leash—what better treat for a dog who'd been cooped up? She took the freedom thing to heart—and took off. It took us ninety minutes to find her and lure her back into the car.

At home, things weren't entirely smooth, either. Maggie was nervous when we fed her, crouching in the corner as if she associated feeding time with getting pummeled. She was clearly anxious when we left her alone. She warmed up to us quickly, but there were other issues. We were in the habit of meeting other "dog people" at the neighborhood park down the road, where locals chatted over coffee while the dogs played. Most of the time Maggie did fine. But, true to her alpha nature and what we guessed was some sort of herding dog heritage, she tended to round up and dominate any dog who would let her. There were a few incidents when herding would suddenly escalate into a fight, and pretty soon I started keeping her on the leash and avoiding that park. We went for long walks instead and explored Cambridge, Massachusetts, where we lived at the time.

It also became clear that she hated to be left behind in unfamiliar surroundings. When we left her at my parents' house to go out in their boat for a couple of hours, she jumped onto a four-foot windowsill, jimmied the screen off, and scampered down the hill. She was pacing on the dock when we got back. On a trip to visit relatives in New Jersey, we took her out one night and left her in the car to avoid destruction to my in-laws' home. In the midst of a cold beer and a pool game, Maggie turned up in the bar. She had somehow turned the hand crank on the sunroof (which we'd left open a crack for air) enough to escape out the top, then nudged open the screen door of the small country bar.

We dealt with the separation anxiety and Houdini tendencies, but then came new issues. About a year later, after we had moved one town over to a second-floor apartment, my husband and I learned I was pregnant with twins. Maggie had already recently had a rough transition to her new home, where it seemed to bother her that she couldn't see the street, and where she found a small white terrier in the neighborhood particularly distasteful. If that transition was rough, what would it be like to add two babies to the mix?

Our strategy: Be prepared. I sought out a professional trainer who specialized in aggressive dogs. He taught me to work with her instincts, told me she needed a "job," and that we needed to assume control as the head honchos of her "pack" at home. We worked hard with him every week, and faithfully practiced our lessons twice a day. We played tapes of crying babies to get her used to the sound. When the girls were born, my husband brought back some of their tiny hospital clothes so Maggie could get

used to their smell before they arrived. Our preparation paid off;
Maggie was wonderful with the babies, accepting them into the
fold without question. She slept by their cribs at night in the room
next to ours and walked with me twice a day alongside the stroller.

Trouble was, she took her new role as mother's helper a
little too seriously, becoming more protective of her pack than

Maggie

ever. She seemed to feel an expanded
responsibility for keeping any
questionable visitors in line and would
especially follow men around, walking
right at their heels. On occasion, she'd
nip at the backs of their knees. In
hindsight, these were red flags we
should have taken more seriously, if it
weren't for the complete sleep deficit
and overwhelming nature of life with twin infants.

When our girls were eighteen months old, we left urban
Massachusetts for small-town life on the Maine coast. Maggie,
we figured, would thrive here too, with a two-acre yard to roam
in and a comfortable house instead of a cramped second-floor
apartment. Wrong again. Instead of reveling in the space and
quiet, it seemed to overwhelm her. It was as if there was too much
turf to guard and protect and she couldn't possibly cover it all.

What's more, our daughters were no longer infants in bassinets. They had to be tracked, too, and they were constantly moving, often in opposite directions.

Early after the move, Maggie had two more significant clashes with other dogs. Neither was her fault, but their impact got added to the growing number of upsetting incidents in her troubled life. First, a tiny white terrier attacked Maggie from its yard while we walked by, two babies in the jogger and all. Maggie responded by picking her up by the neck and shaking the terrier violently. I watched in horror, along with the other owner—neither of us could figure out how to intervene—but amazingly, the terrier was unharmed. In the second incident, Maggie was caught off guard by a giant mastiff, who bounded around the corner of a trail and went right for her—luckily, she fought off his charge without serious injury.

We hired another trainer. We tried a low-protein diet designed to lower her energy levels. We experimented with various collars. Gave her "jobs" by having her fetch and learn more commands. Nothing solved her issues.

I don't know what provoked Maggie to snap at our daughter. We were all in the family room, with Maggie and the girls on the floor in front of the couch. Out of the blue, she turned and quickly snapped her jaws on one of the girls' legs. No blood, no broken skin, but a line had clearly been crossed. Although I knew what had to happen, I felt terribly guilty. I couldn't help but feel that we'd let her down, and that it just wasn't fair for us to play God with her life. I spoke with our vet. I spoke with two more trainers. Matt and I went over all the options, but none of them seemed realistic—after all, how could we put her back in another shelter, or find new owners who would adopt a troubled dog? I cried a lot. And I made an appointment to have her put to sleep.

When the dreaded day arrived a week later, I dropped the girls off at our sitter's house and drove with Maggie to the vet. She walked in, completely trusting of me, and minutes later got stuck with a needle. I left in a wash of tears and haven't been able to set foot in that vet's office again.

As I write this, my eyes are brimming over again as the guilt and sadness return, fresh as if this were yesterday instead of six years ago. Even though we had to do what we did for our family and others' safety, I don't think I'll ever feel right about ending her life. The vet sent her ashes to us. They are still sitting in our hall closet. I haven't been able to bring myself to bury her.

Two years later, we got another dog, whose family had seen one too many trash cans dumped over and had little time to exercise him enough. Trapper was another grownup, also black, a certified Lab. But because we knew Trapper's family, this time the history was there to see, not a wild guess. He has his warts: Left to his own devices, he'll eat unlimited quantities of anything from zucchini to birdseed. He likes to bark at the FedEx guy, which instantly sends me into fits of worry that he'll bite someone and we'll be repeating history. But still, in a way, Trapper helps to lessen my guilt over Maggie—I feel redeemed to think we're giving another dog a home that needed one. I understand his straightforward dog ways, and for the most part, if you tire him out enough, he's manageable and predictable in a way that Maggie never would be. Maybe this time we're getting it right.

Trading Spaces
Kathryn Renner

Charlie Brown had the right idea: Build a little house
outside for the dog. Let him contemplate the grass, the
sky, and his bird friends and be deliciously happy. But more often
than not, today's best friend lives underfoot, not alfresco. Catalogs
and doggy boutiques tout beds for Bowzer that fit any decorating
theme: a flannel bed with a built-in heater for the cabin, or for the
boudoir, a mini-canopy reminiscent of Versailles.

Our dachshund, Murphy Brown, has gone one better.
Murphy B. has claimed our '99 Mercedes 320E—leather seats,
sunroof, lumbar support and all.

Her craving for finer digs began when we were remodeling
the house. Foolhardy that we were, we chose to inhabit one
depressing corner of the basement while workers yanked out pipes

and ripped down doors. We reminded ourselves (hourly) that living like cave dwellers and resisting a stay at the Holiday Inn saved us a bundle.

Murphy B. had no such frame of reference. All she knew was that strangers were in her space. As soon as the drills and hammers started their racket, she flattened her ears and cowered behind the spindly leg of our one makeshift table.

Murphy B.

So shortly after the remodel began, we decided to put her in the car. Once safe inside, she immediately curled her peanut body up on the contoured seats and fell into dreams of off-leash parks. Surrounded by noise, fumes, a haze of Sheetrock dust, and radios blaring country music, Murphy B. escaped the racket every day and snoozed as if she were wearing Bose headphones, thanks to solid German engineering. She brought new meaning to "asleep behind the wheel."

Months later, we moved into our new space, ready to share it with Murphy B. But she had other ideas.

That was three years ago.

These days, Murphy B. loves to come out of her vehicle for

two meals and a walk daily. She adores it when her car moves. We call it running errands, but for her it's snacking in bed, since the drive-thru bank teller, under the influence of Murphy B's stare, sends out liver treats in the pneumatic tube.

Yes, Murphy B. still joins us inside on occasion. She has two beds: One is lined with her favorite seafoam green, Pennsylvania Dutch–patterned quilt, the other has the softest sheepskin cushion, most likely from the underbellies of beasts that graze in the remote Andes.

But after tolerating these beds as long as she can, she works hard to get our attention. (Think Lassie trying to tell the doctor that Timmy is injured in the forest.) When we finally follow her, she makes a beeline for the door. Not the front door, where her leash is, but the door to the garage. She freezes and points her body like an exclamation point, divining us to open that door. If we ignore her, she sulks. If we indulge her, she scampers to the Mercedes, a hot dog wriggling with delight. "I'd feel sorry for her spending so much time in there," says our son, "except she's so happy!"

While we sit on our deck overlooking the backyard (where a doghouse should be) we know where Murphy B. is: snoring with limbs splayed across the leather seats, content as Snoopy has ever been. . . .

Dog Days
on the Farm
Sarah Shey

My parents' farm was never without a dog. The dog was as much a part of the landscape as the garden overrun with zucchini or the yard light punctuating the darkness. Farm dogs weren't coddled creatures. They did not wear monogrammed raincoats or polka-dotted ribbons. They did not sleep on goose-down ticks or velvet beanbags. They were not privy to airplane rides or massages. They were pampered only when my family took vacations: A neighbor lady provided pickup rides down the gravel road to her house. But they were loved—as one loves someone who is always there.

I found dogs much easier to figure out than my two sisters. The youngest of three boys and three girls, I arrived fifteen years after Jane, the firstborn, and eight years after Carla. Around them, I was the crowd: the tagalong, never the leader, the copier, never

the copied, the brat, never the mature one—a bona fide gadfly.
For years, I tried to catch up with my sisters. For years, it seemed I
never would.

But I never felt like a gadfly with our farm dogs—nor did I
ever have to try. On the cattle, corn, and bean farm near the county
seat town of Algona, Iowa, being with dogs was almost instinctual.
Dogs appreciated fresh water, scraps from the kitchen table—
preferably slices of bread soaked in juices from a roast—and dog
food, which they waited to eat until they were alone. Dogs needed
their coats shaved once a year to remove their mud skirts. Ticks
had to be plucked before they plumped into tomatoes of blood.
Petting was enjoyed anytime.

My parents did not discuss the merits of owning a farm dog.
It was just something you did. It was how they were both raised.
Since I was the youngest, I had missed out on Lassie #1, Lassie #2
and Lassie #3—all collies, of course—but survived the reigns of
Treva, Missy, Molly, and Shelby. Even though they were farm dogs,
they did not have to work hard. Our hired hand, Ed, preferred
to be alone. The dogs' main responsibilities were barking at
unfamiliar pickups and helping when bovine escaped from a cattle
lot to the fields. Otherwise, the dogs dug holes, tracked skunks, or
visited our neighbors when bored. But with a large family around,
the dogs kept busy—or made efforts to appear so.

Lassie #2, who resembled the movie star, had a talent for slaying rabbits and dropping them at my mother's feet. Lassie #3, another movie star clone, was known to guide Carla around the yard by her coat sleeve when she was a toddler. Treva, a short-haired German shepherd–collie mix, snipped at my ankles when I rode my bike, causing me to cry and pedal very fast. Missy, an outgoing collie, held barkathons with neighboring hounds. Molly, a gentle, maternal type, accompanied me when I bottle-fed Ajax, an orphan calf. Shelby, a white border collie with black eyes, bullied cats as our car pulled into the yard, hoping to appear indispensable. The dogs—a dog—were always around, always there for me. Sisters were another story.

At age five, I did what I could to curry favor. Each week, I wrote a letter on lined stationary to Jane, who was away at college in Sioux City, Iowa, three hours away from the farm. They were variations of, "I watered the cats and dog. Sheila McGuire and me played school. Mom and me made cookies. WRITE BACK NOW."

I used a less subtle method on Carla. Each day, I followed her around the house. If she watched TV, helped Mom make dinner, ate mashed potatoes with gravy, or listened to the soundtrack of *Pippin*, I did too.

Their reactions were emblematic of their personalities. Jane never wrote back, even after my last entreaty, which threatened a cease-and-desist of future letters if she failed to reply. She proffered stuffed animals instead. I was unable to see those as a type of letter for me. Carla, on the other hand, never appreciated that imitation was a great form of flattery and wrote in her diary, which I found in her secret hiding place, between two sweaters in her cedar chest: "I HATE SARAH. SHE FOLLOWS ME EVERYWHERE. SHE COPIES EVERYTHING I DO. SHE'S CHUBBY, TOO!" "Hate" was underlined not once but four times. I gasped. "What are you doing with my diary?" Carla shrieked. She yanked the book from me and I scampered off, seeking an audience with the family dog.

Shelby

During almost every predicament—prosaic or otherwise—I took solace in a dog's coat. Missy, who had luxurious fur, hid with me in the machine shed while the rest of my family raked leaves. She perched beside me after I returned from school upset that a classmate had called me fat (a gross miscalculation; technically, I was chubby). She was there when I contemplated the word "hate."

A Catholic schoolgirl, I, along with my classmates, was always encouraged to use the word dislike instead, because the

H-word should only be applied to serious situations: the devil, drugs, disease, famine, war. Was I a serious situation? I sighed and dropped my face into Missy's coat, inhaling her signature scent: cattle with manure cutting through, followed by a second course of skunk, finished with farm air. I decided that a dog was the perfect sister: close in age (in dog years), nonjudgmental about my appearance, and a lover of tagalongs.

That night, I did Carla's supper chores: cleared the table, dried the dishes and put them away. Carla let me sing a duet with her from *Fiddler on the Roof* before we fell asleep. I had been forgiven.

Too bad our dogs could never participate in such late-night theater. My mother didn't allow them in the house.

"They're outdoor animals," she sniffed. "That's where they belong."

But when my parents drove off for the evening, to sip old-fashioneds in one of their friend's carpeted living rooms, dogs became our guests—unwilling ones, I admit.

Our dogs weren't like our cats, who sneaked in at every chance, waiting for the moment when the screen door slowed down to its nine-second pause before banging shut. Dogs had to be dragged in. This was why I decided dogs were better than cats. Dogs knew they weren't allowed inside, that there were consequences to trespassing. Cats, selfish creatures that they were, did not care.

As I reached for Molly with both of my hands—as if greeting a long-lost relative—she backed up and began to look worried. I clasped both my arms around her and half-carried and half-dragged her into the back entrance. She landed over the threshold with a thump. Then she looked left and right, with that worried look.

"It's okay, doggy," I said. "Mom and Dad are gone and they will never know."

It was a thrill to have Molly indoors. I brushed her hair, dressed her in my mother's church hats, and told her epic tales about dogs on horses. She seemed flattered by the attention. Then my brother Doug rushed in. "Headlights!"

Headlights!

We worked quickly. We positioned ourselves behind Molly, as if to push a stalled car, and shoved her back over the threshold to—*thump*—the outdoors. We locked the front door and scooted upstairs to try to appear innocent when our parents checked in on us. It was the perfect crime—we didn't hurt anyone or deface any property—and we didn't need to worry about a canine informant.

Dogs were always up for anything, save for my mother's house rules—they weren't really "no" creatures, a word children heard a lot. So when this dog, who seemed to love you even more than your sisters and brothers and parents combined, had an accident, it was devastating. Farm dogs' hazards were few but violent. When farmers mowed their fields in the summer, dogs sometimes ran along, nipping at the machine so closely that a leg would get chewed up and need to be amputated. That never happened to one of our dogs, but they experienced their share of misfortunes. A batch of puppies was kidnapped from the corncrib and never seen again. Treva was put to sleep for being nasty. The last straw was snarling at Ed, making him hop onto a station wagon.

Moving vehicles were farm dogs' main predators. Lassie #3 was struck by a grain truck but lived to bark his tale. Ten days after my veterinarian father pinned the broken bone, Lassie leaned against the barn and pulled the pin out so he could do laps to strengthen his leg. Lassie #2 was killed in a hit-and-run accident; Jane discovered him by the mailbox when the family returned from Sunday brunch.

Missy met death this way, too. I saw it happen. At around 5:00 PM, Ed rumbled down our farm road in his mufferless pickup, Missy chasing him. Many farm dogs ran after vehicles; Missy was no different.

"Missy, come!" I yelled. I leaned against the swing set and waited for her to turn around. But she didn't. Instead, she stretched her paws forward, took ground with her, and stretched her paws forward again—past the bend in the lane, past the tree where the raccoons lived.

At the asparagus-rhubarb patch, I saw something peculiar: Missy seemed to be racing against the back wheels. Somehow she got ahead of the wheel. Maybe Ed swerved to miss a pothole, or maybe Missy tripped, but the wheel caught her and threw her down. Ed drove away, unaware of what had happened.

"Missy!" I screamed. I sprinted over. For an instant I noticed a spark in her eyes, then darkness. I laid my body on hers and felt her warm body, her coat of soft hair. She didn't seem to be dead.

I ran to the house.

"Dad!" I screamed. "Mom, where's Dad?" She stopped peeling potatoes in the kitchen sink.

"In the basement," she said.

I clomped down the stairs and found my dad shrugging on a pair of clean coveralls.

"Ed ran over Missy! Hurry!" I hopped up two stairs at a time and burst into the yard, back to our dog, who hadn't moved.

My breath came quickly. My stomach ached.

My father touched her neck.

"Sarah, she's dead."

"No. No! She was alive a bit ago. I saw her eyes; they were awake. Do something!"

But he couldn't. His vet degree didn't include bringing pets back from the dead.

My father and I buried her in an unmarked grave in the grove. I sprinkled dandelions over the upturned earth and said a prayer for her.

That night, I walked toward the sunset, down the gravel road that I usually shared with Missy, where she pranced ahead, stopped, looked at me, and then pranced onward.

I avoided Ed for days, making him feel worse.

We eventually got another collie. My parents answered an ad in the newspaper and drove to an amateur breeder and picked out a promising pup. We named her Molly. She was little. She was cute. Life moved on.

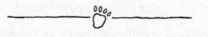

I began to get along better with my sisters when I grew up. In a gradual epiphany, I realized a major benefit of families. Among all the unpredictable things in life, you could at least count on a few predictable people, who possessed similar idiosyncrasies: recycling tin foil by pressing it into squares; making peanut butter sandwiches with a redundant layer of butter; eating corn on the cob typewriter style. Which was why I treasured our dogs. They were predictable: They always had the good manners to wag their tails hello—no matter how much time had passed since your last visit.

You don't learn this, though, until you leave home. I took a lot for granted—my family, the farm, the dogs—until I moved to New York for graduate school. Although I felt displaced, I knew that you couldn't stay at home, shoving your dog over the threshold, forever.

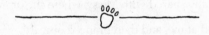

In New York, my days in Iowa seemed to belong to another century—so different was the way of life, the topography, the people, the dogs. The dogs! One day, I traipsed down Fifth Avenue and witnessed two men walking twelve dogs, six to a person, three in each hand. Dog walkers! I gawked. A leashed dog represented a startling other type of lifestyle. That poor Great Dane, I sighed, watching it trot by and imagining its apartment. On another day, I noticed a Maltese wearing a cashmere sweater (from Barneys, no doubt).

But the morning in Central Park when I met a three-legged French bulldog and her owner was the day I wondered how I'd ever make it in New York. I slowed down as the five-legged pair approached. My friend Greg, a former New Yorker, had admonished me about talking to strangers before my move—he feared for a farmer's daughter. But a woman with a dog seemed like a chance to make a pleasant—and much-needed—connection, to speak about a subject I liked.

"Oh, what happened?" I asked the owner. She was a severe-looking woman with dyed black hair and white eyebrows that made her look perpetually alarmed. Keeping my distance, I bent down and placed my palm up for the dog to smell.

"You'll have to ask Uma," she said, and gestured to her dog. The owner tipped her nose to the sky and left me there, watching them saunter away.

I felt like I had been slapped on the nose.

I boarded the bus back to the Upper West Side. A storm loomed in the sky, the little I could see of it among the tall buildings. Walking down West 115th Street, I passed John Lennon, a potbellied pig who lived next door, and ducked into my apartment's foyer just as the rain fell. I climbed the four flights of stairs and flopped onto my sofa, yearning for some dog fur to make me feel better. I felt more alone than I had during my one-month stay.

But I would never have a dog in a New York apartment. They were outdoor animals. They needed to spend time in the fresh air, sniffing curlicue patterns across the lawn, chasing squirrels up trees, digging bothersome holes, teasing cats. They needed to be autonomous, relying on someone only for food and affection and a doghouse. A division between the indoors and the outdoors needed to exist, I agreed with my mother—a reason for my children to one day sneak our dog into the house while I'm drinking gin-and-tonics on a friend's front porch.

Case in point: the current family dog Shelby. Shelby was dumped at a vet's office in Humboldt, a town thirty minutes from my parents' farm. My brother Pat, who lived near my parents, adopted her to be a house dog, an arrangement Shelby took literally. She chewed on antiques, dug holes in the carpet, scratched the wood floors.

"Would you consider taking Shelby?" Pat asked our father.

"Who's going to take care of it?" he snapped. It peeved him when people failed to grasp the duties involved in dog care.

One Saturday morning, Pat dropped off Shelby at the farm to exercise. It was as if she had been sprung from prison; she galloped around the farm, wearing a giddy grin—for eight hours. Every time my brother tried to catch her, she'd sprint away, circle back, and glance at him, bemused, then sprint some more. My parents took pity; she got to stay. She became a regular in the back of my father's red pickup, nose jutting out, in olfactory heaven.

More thunder cracked; rain dripped from the sky. The university-issue sofa was like lounging on cardboard, so I changed into my pajamas and climbed into bed. I imagined what Shelby was doing—on the alert for raccoons. I imagined how I looked from the moon—just a speck curled up in a twin bed, thinking of home.

At Thanksgiving, I flew back to Rural Route #2, meeting my sisters in the Minneapolis airport for the three-hour car ride to the farm. To outsiders, we were a morbid crew. We spoke of death and dying—who had a farm sale; who moved to town; who moved into the rest home; who died. I stared out at the fields topped with crushed dirt and snow and thought of the upcoming weekend and the things we'd do. My mother had once told me about her aunts, her mother's sisters, who liked to visit back and forth. Back then, circa 1940, Mom said, there weren't as many things to do. Family was your social life. Times had not changed our town of six thousand that much; there were no malls, no zoos, no museums. My sisters and I would hand-crank ice cream, drop off cookies at a bachelor farmer's, visit the North Place, forty acres my parents owned two miles north of the farm, and admire a friend's afghan blankets. It would be plenty.

Even though we were often silent in the car, these three

women, who lived in three different quadrants of the country and saw each other only a few times a year, rode together. We got along. Shelby met our car after each outing, stretching her front paws into a curtsy. She seemed content to be on the welcome-home committee, even if she didn't get to tag along. But I made sure to spend time with her. One afternoon I tossed a gift, a squeaky squirrel tail, into the air. Shelby dashed after it, then trotted down the lane. I followed. It was glorious to be back in rural Iowa, a place I understood well: penned pigs, limitless sky, and leashless dogs.

Leaving Our Chains
Susan T. Lennon

Sporting his new training collar, my puppy followed me into our tiny hall bathroom. I'd recently quit my big insurance job, and I adored my new life—as "mom" to a clumsy four-month-old yellow Labrador retriever. Harley is a flash-eyed underpants-stealer, with too-long legs and a too-stout tummy. Absentmindedly I washed up, thinking about the adventures that awaited us today. Yesterday, it was a shredded bed, followed by Harley careening around the living room like a Tasmanian devil and me laughing despite myself.

High-pitched yelping startled me, and the soap slipped from my hands as I realized that Harley was no longer snuffling around my ankles; he was wedged up under the toilet. Squinting, I saw that his metal collar had snagged on the pipe-and-valve fixture down there, and when he tried to break free, the O-ring twisted itself over and around. With every move he made, the links tightened into a hangman's noose.

Cold waves of panic surged through me as I knelt beside him, trying to figure out what to do. Cursing the trainer who'd insisted that Harley wear the collar, and myself for hiring her, I dropped to my knees for a closer look, blathering reassurances so he wouldn't struggle and make the situation worse. He was panting, and his soft brown eyes rolled white with fear, imploring me to help. I crouched beside him, clueless. I knew nothing of plumbing, never mind saving a life.

Scrunching my eyes shut, I hoped for one of those adrenaline-crazed, superhuman, ultra maternal bursts of strength you read about. Bare-handed, I first attempted to pull the pipe from the wall and then, when that didn't work, tried to break the chain apart.

I failed. I needed help.

"It's gonna be okay, baby," I whispered as I got up and rushed to the kitchen phone. Grabbing the handset, I took a deep breath and punched in three numbers.

An operator answered, "This is 911. State your emergency, please."

My sweaty hand could barely hold the phone as I blurted, "You've got to help, my puppy is trapped under the toilet, choking . . . he'll die . . . send somebody, quick!"

"Uh, who exactly is gonna die?"

"My *dog*."

I couldn't believe my ears when she responded, "Ma'am, we don't do dogs. We're strictly a human rescue. Call someone else."

My response can still make me blush, but at the time I didn't even hesitate. "Listen, if you don't get out here, you *will* have a human emergency on your hands! I'll have a heart attack or a breakdown if anything happens to him!" Then I slammed down the phone and rushed back to Harley, slipping my finger between the chain and his neck so he could breathe. My heart was pounding. This couldn't be happening.

I'd long wanted a dog, and daydreamed about it during the last miserable months of my high-pressure corporate job. I could no longer handle the continuous strain of competition, the perpetual need to watch my back, and the ongoing pseudodrama of insurance minutiae. After eight years of trying to adapt, the stress had taken its toll. I just didn't fit in. I was scared, but I wanted to start my own writing business, get healthy, and simplify my life. With a dog, I explained to my dumbstruck husband, I could set up shop at home, and success would be guaranteed—because how could I leave our dog home alone every day?

Shortly after I quit my job, I carried my squirming, ten-week-old furball home—and soon my headaches fled, my intestines untwisted, and my nails started to grow.

Harley became my lifeline, tugging me back to a contented, pantyhose-free world, one where nurturing, trust, and playfulness ruled. I couldn't even contemplate going back—Harley needed me.

The feeling was mutual.

Harley

My husband had recently remarked, with a smirk, that I'd smiled more in the weeks since this blond boy joined us than I had during the past decade. I wanted to do everything right for him. To take my mind off worrying about whether I could make a living as a home-based writer, I devoured books and articles about caring for a canine. I spent every waking moment with him, reveling in his doggy-ness, seeing the world through his eyes, inhaling the scent of his ruff as if it were an aphrodisiac. I sang him to sleep, dangling my fingers into his crate. And despite my husband's rolling eyes, I even hired a professional trainer to teach me about how to raise a well-adjusted dog.

Click! The trainer insisted that Harley wear this steel trap of a choke collar, claiming that it was the only way to "correct" his behavior as he grew. "You have to show him who's boss," she said.

Sitting on the cold tile, trying not to cry, it hit me that this metal collar and its strong-arm training dogma reflected everything I'd grown to loathe about my job—and what I'd allowed my life to become. Harley didn't need a shackle to jerk him into submission, just as I didn't need to prove my worth by accepting the choke chain of other people's expectations.

But what if we couldn't escape? In some weird way, both of our lives seemed to be at stake here. If I couldn't save Harley, my feelings of grief and failure would force me back to the world I'd so newly left. It seems overly dramatic now, but I felt that if I couldn't even take care of a puppy, I'd never be able to find my way. And at thirty-eight, I wasn't exactly a kid anymore—it seemed like this was my only chance.

Doorbell! I begged Harley to be calm and raced down the hall. Flinging the door open to a pair of burly police, I hustled them toward the bathroom, guns and gear clanking as I babbled.

One guy hunkered down to assess the situation. I sucked in my breath as his rough hands maneuvered Harley's head away from the fixture. He looked over at me and asked for a wrench. My feet were glued to the floor—I honestly didn't even know what a wrench was. Raising an eyebrow, his partner lumbered off to the squad car to get one, and when he returned, he handed it over with an exaggerated sigh. Expertly, Harley's rescuer shut off the water, removed the valve head, and waved the collar aloft in mock victory. They were laughing at me, but I didn't care. We were free.

I picked Harley up and held him as we sunk into the couch. After he settled down, our eyes locked. Wordless communication with another species is potent. I felt like we both knew that somehow we'd just saved each other, and that the bond we'd created through those agonizing moments would change us.

Harley is ten now, and we were right. My dream of a simpler, home-based writing business came true, and during these years, Harley and I have spent endless hours together. We are happy animals, appreciating the moment, still leaving our chains behind.

Once a Dog Mom, Always a Dog Mom

Megan Mc Morris

For my first thirty-two years of life, I stood solidly in the land of cat. I admired their independence, their ability to clean themselves, and their aloof "I'm going to pretend that I don't care if you're in the same room but I really do" nature. Dogs, on the other hand, have always neatly fit into the category I reserved—and still sometimes do reserve—for kids: Fun to play with, yes, but I haven't necessarily wanted to live with them. They drool, jump up on you, are messy and smelly, and I thought their always-eager, uncouth attitude proved that cats were more sophisticated.

Dogs were also pretty scary: My most frightening childhood memories inevitably involved some member of the canine family—from the infamous dog next door who I'd have nightmares about (you know the ones, where you're being chased and suddenly your legs do that slow motion dream-running thing) to the barking German shepherds who would leer menacingly (or so I thought) at my eight-year-old self as I walked to school.

As you're probably guessing by now, this all changed when I met a certain furry someone—a nine-year-old Siberian husky named Corvus after the star constellation for the black crow.

I became a dog owner because of the local police: After Corvus's outdoor kennel mate died at her grandparents' house, she was causing a minor ruckus howling from loneliness every day, and her neighbors—and, therefore, the police—weren't quite feeling the love. Something had to be done. Her dad, whom I was living with at the time, decided to take her in. He'd officially owned her from birth, but she had been living with his parents for the past few years because they had a big yard on the river for her to roam on, whereas he'd lived in an apartment in Portland. We'd recently moved to a converted barn in Hood River, with a huge meadow (complete with sheep and horses!), so it was perfect timing for her to join her dad again.

Our first night as roommates went a little something like this: I was trying to sleep, while she snacked on a bone. Loudly. Her dad was obliviously snoring next to me and was no help, so I decided to take her bone away from her, placing it above my head on the bookshelf. She stared at me and there was an intense *mano-a-mano* moment where I thought she would go for my throat; those "dogs are scary" feelings aren't so easily erased. Instead, she blinked at me, then curled up on her bed and closed her eyes. It was my first hint that maybe she wasn't a woman-eating beast after all.

But I didn't truly turn the dog corner until we began our hiking adventures. By a happy coincidence, I was just about to embark on a year of massive hiking in preparation for a guidebook I was writing. I desperately needed some help logging all those miles, and a hiking companion would also keep me safe and sane. Turns out, I had found just the buddy.

Our first hike together happened just a few weeks after we became roommates. I had never even walked a dog with a leash before, so I had a lot to learn. I also had a lot to learn about hiking and trail-finding, I quickly discovered, after we ended up missing our trail turnoff and trekking too far into the wilderness—and through snow. To make a long story somewhat short, we ended up having to backtrack in the dark for two hours with no flashlight. While I would have been nervous to be out there alone, I felt like she and I were in this together, and she handled it like a pro. Her fluffy, wagging white tail picked up the moonlight and acted as a beacon for me as she led me back like a true sled dog. Calm, cool, and collected, she automatically turned the right way at each of the many trail junctions (now *that's* something a cat wouldn't do!), and she waited patiently for me every time I fell behind. By the time we got back to the trailhead, a major bond had formed. During those five hours of hiking, I had become a dog mom.

When we got back to our warm house, with a glass of red wine for me and a big bowl of cold water for her, Corvus placed herself at my feet with her head facing the door. I didn't think anything of that, until her dad commented that she was sitting there on purpose; she was protecting me! Needless to say, that sealed the deal for me.

Corvus

Fast forward three years and many hiking adventures—and mishaps—later, and I'd entered a world from which there's no return: the world of dog. It's such a different arena than the feline world, that it caught me off-guard at first. My maternal instincts appeared in ways I never imagined. I suddenly understood how much pleasure you can get when you're truly responsible for someone else's happiness (whether that "someone else" has fur or not), and I got a distinct sense of pride when I watched Corvie twirl around three times as she plumped up her circular dog bed with her paw before collapsing onto it with a dramatic sigh. I craved her company when I was away from her, talked about her so much I made my childless, dogless sister roll her eyes too many times to count.

My maternal pride materialized in the simplest of ways. Just walking down the street from my Northwest Portland apartment turned into a public display of Corvus. I'm not one to mosey; if I'm going somewhere, I walk as fast as I can to get there. (Eight years in The Big Apple will do that to you.) But with a dog, my walks turned from brisk gotta-get-there strides to slow meanders, stopping at every bush or garbage can so C. could check out who had been there before her. She loved going on errands with me, because it was like a walking buffet, complete with a pepperoni stick at the corner store on 23rd and Thurman—where the owner would personally tear it into bite-sized chunks and feed it to her, commenting on her "good table manners." I beamed as if I had personally taught her how to gently take food from outstretched hands.

Walking was Corvie's turn to shine, and she wasn't shy: She would strut down the street like a rock star with an attitude, tail high. When we went past the windows of neighborhood restaurants, it would never fail: heads swiveled, fingers pointed, faces smiled. People would literally run after me on the street or call out from their cars: What type of dog? How old is she? What's her name? I suddenly understood what it would feel like to be a parent; no one cared about me, it was her they wanted to talk to and look at, and I didn't mind one bit.

Off the public runway, I also tasted parenthood, for better or worse. My daily life started revolving around her needs. As a magazine writer, I do a lot of phone interviews. Before I started dialing, I would prepare C. so she was walked and fed and, ideally, quiet. But it was never that easy. Usually, she simply didn't like that my attention wasn't going to her. I'd see the familiar progression and wince: I'd be on the phone and notice her looking at me. Once our eyes locked, she would sit up and start pacing, as she geared up for a big husky *Woo!* (she definitely had a flair for the dramatic). I would pull out the only parenting trick I knew: Distraction. I'd head straight for the kitchen, one hand clutching a notepad and pen, the phone cradled in my shoulder, as I got her treat out, trying to maintain a somewhat professional tone with the person on the other end. Then I'd lead her back to her bed, pat it so she'd sit, and give her a treat or three to keep her busy. For the first time, I understood what parents on planes feel like when you're doing everything you can think of to prevent a crying fit.

Having a dog filled some type of need I didn't know I had. I've always been someone who needs plenty of alone time, and even though I work by myself every day, I still need a couple nights a week entirely to myself or I start to get twitchy and irritated. But with a dog, I experienced a new sense of aloneness. Suddenly it was like being alone, yet not. Being alone, only better, having someone to turn to during commercials of *America's Next Top Model* and say "Congratulations, Corvus, you're still in the running toward becoming America's Next Top Model Dog." Upon hearing her name, she'd raise her head to look at me with one ice-blue eye and one chocolate-brown eye—a feature sure to grab the judges' attention—before she put her head back down and sighed, as if relieved to still be in the running. I started envisioning myself as an old lady, a dog curled up at my side on the couch. With apologies to Lily, my brown tabby cat, I realized that being a dog lady rather than a cat lady had a nicer ring to it. Plus, it gave me a better answer to that tiring "You gonna have kids?" question.

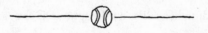

Was. Weren't. Used to. Did. There's a reason I've been using the past tense.

"I lost custody," is my short-and-sweet explanation for those who ask, hoping they'll drop the subject and won't go on about how beautiful she was (is), how they loved when she *Woo*ed, and how they'll miss her, as I nod and smile and say in one rushed breath, "well she is eleven years old and she's well taken care of now," as my throat constricts and my face flushes. My breakup with Corvus and her dad was tough on all of us and is something I'm not comfortable talking about to just anyone. For a long time, I thought visitation rights would work, until I realized that in order for me to go on with my life—something all of my friends agreed was long overdue—I needed to cut the cord. Otherwise, letting Corvus stay with me at my new apartment meant that her dad was in my life more than he should have been, and as comfortable as that little family unit sometimes was that we'd created, it couldn't work if I was going to move on. I had to just let go.

Lily, for one, was overjoyed when she realized she now got to rule the roost without two big dog eyes following her every move. I imagine her with her left paw outstretched, "jazz paw" style, right paw holding her tail as a microphone as she sidesteps across the living room, belting out the "Freedom" refrain from Aretha Franklin's "Think" at the top of her kitty voice. No more creeping around the room's perimeters at a glacial pace toward me so as not to attraction attention from the dog; now, she can leap and jump right in the middle of the living room when she gets the urge to play. No more curtailed visits on my lap because the dog gets jealous and suddenly has to go outside.

I could relate: I had been so All Dog, All The Time. I had

braced myself for how hard it was going to be without Corvus, but then a surprising thing happened: My overriding feeling was relief and a newfound sense of freedom. Obviously, it was mainly to do with how I felt about cutting the cord from her dad, which made me feel free in a way I hadn't felt in the previous four years with him, but it was also to do with not having *any* responsibility. Suddenly, I could go wherever I wanted—with whomever I wanted—and not have to worry about anything. I could get up whenever I felt the urge, instead of bolting upright as soon as she woke up so she wouldn't howl and wake my neighbors. I could hold a phone conversation without having to dash around the kitchen offering up bribes so she'd be quiet. And I could stay out as late as I wanted without having to worry about anyone's full bladder except my own. Lily tries to give me her best beady-eyed stare when I'm out too long, but she doesn't hold a grudge—as long as her food and water bowl are filled and I sit down long enough for her to knead and purr on my lap, she's a happy camper.

Of course, that's just the eternally optimistic side of me. The other side, the one I try to hide behind my rushed explanation of why "it's okay, *really*," that I don't have my dog anymore is the one that misses her every day. The mom in me.

To distract myself, I've become a fairy dogmother of sorts, a job that keeps me busy. Now, instead of one, I have about fifty to check in on. They don't know I'm looking in on them, but I like to think they can sense that they, too, are loved.

My dogmother responsibilities began a few months after I had lost custody of Corvus, when my new boyfriend, Eric, emailed me. The subject line was just one word: "Duuuuude!" I opened it to a listing from the Oregon Humane Society in which a bug-eyed Australian cattle dog/shepherd mix named Tony looked up at me. His eager face took up the whole picture (I think they angle pictures this way on purpose to maximize cuteness potential), and his description only furthered the adorable factor: "Tony is a little nervous here, and he's unsure about walking on slick surfaces."

Tony's paws become an inside joke between us: "Well, you know Tony's afraid of those slick surfaces, wouldn't he like to come to my apartment where there's carpeting?" We laughed about whether the adoption form specifically asked whether you have carpet (because, well, you know Tony). We joked about buying little booties and dropping them off at the shelter with a note. "Hi, these are for Tony until he gains more confidence on those slick surfaces."

As much as it was a joke, though, I realized I was also becoming attached to seeing his adorable photo. I started not only checking in on Tony, but also on his fellow shelter buddies while I was cruising the website. It became a sort of hobby—until one day I checked in on Tony and burst into tears at his eager eyes looking up at me. I realized I now had a habit.

Over breakfast a few weeks after the weeping episode he said, "I think we need to go see Tony today." He hadn't mentioned it before, but I imagined there was a piece of him that felt somehow responsible for my dogless status; after all, separating fully from Corvus's dad was precipitated by my relationship with Eric.

On the way to the shelter, I couldn't believe that I was actually going to see Tony live and in person. I imagined him looking up at me, panting with excitement, and—dare I dream?—physically leaning his little dog body into my legs to get closer to me. I'm such a sucker for the leaners of the canine world.

Instead, once we got to his cage, he was fast asleep. Among all the barking and excitement of busy-visiting-day Saturday, he was snoozing without a care in the world. "But Tony," I wanted to say, "it's *me!*" We peered into his cage, both of us not wanting to admit that we were disappointed. Eventually, he woke up . . . and he looked different than his picture—not as helpless, bigger, almost aggressive.

"His tail is all stubby," Eric tilted his head as he inspected Tony's behind.

"Yeah, that's how the breed is," I responded, feeling

protective. Even though he was now alert, he was barely interested in us; he was more concerned with ferociously barking at the dog being walked down the aisle.

"It's like when you're in jail and all the guys are teasing the new fish," Eric said to lighten the mood. I laughed weakly.

We moved on.

Walking down the row of cages was like going to a reunion—I felt like the dogs were all old friends. "Oh, Jax is still here, he's been here since June, poor guy!" Or, "Oh, there's Dewey, wow, he's much cuter in person without that silly crown on his head in his picture!" When we got to the cage of Cisco the husky, I started tearing up; his white fluffy tail, multicolored eyes, and snowy white coat brushed with black reminded me of C. After I got over my flush of emotion, though, I took a closer look. Cisco's body was thinner, his tail more ragged, and he barely looked me in the eye.

Next to Cisco was a German shepherd mix named Shirley, and we both fell for her floppy cream-colored ears and athletic body. We decided to play with her, and amid the excitement in the "get acquainted" room, where she ran around and squeaked with happiness as we chased her, I realized that I'd forever be comparing dogs to Corvus—kind of like when you're in rebound mode and are comparing all guys to your ex-boyfriend, and no one quite lives up to the mold until you're officially over him.

We left without a dog.

That trip made me realize I wasn't ready to be a dog mom again. But I was conflicted nevertheless: As much as I enjoyed my newfound freedom, I felt guilty at leaving empty-handed. It was misplaced guilt at not seeing Corvus, I know, but guilt nonetheless.

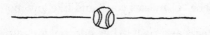

Even though I'm not ready to start attending to a dog's every need, I still check the website as religiously as one might check stock quotes. It's updated so often I practically get real-time results, a la SportsLine during March Madness. I make bets about how long certain animals will stay there—the Chihuahua was a goner in a day (a no-brainer), and the puffball dogs barely have to set their dainty paws in their cages before they're snatched up.

"There was a shipment of Saint Bernard puppies in the other day; they got adopted within a day," I announce to Eric over sushi one night, gesturing with my chopsticks. "But what's the deal with them taking that new young Lab to the pet store for an outreach event, like he wouldn't be adopted anyway? What about the Jaxes and Deweys of the world, the ones who have been there since *June?*" I ask, practically grabbing him by the lapel. Luckily, he likes hearing what he calls the "daily soap opera" of the humane society, and looking at all of the cute dog listings I send him at work. (Or if he doesn't, at least he humors me.)

————————— ✺ —————————

As I write this, it's been three months since I've seen C. or talked to her dad. I'm afraid that if I talk to him, the first words out of his mouth will be "C. misses you," and like any mother would, I'd break into tears and rush to her side, opening up a situation that's best left shut. I like to think of her as having a good life. I don't want to think about her wondering where I went. I hope that dogs don't think that way, that they just adapt to their new surroundings. Don't they?

Once I'm ready to take on more responsibility than a daily Meow Mix and litter scoop, I'll slip back into the dog mom world again. As for whether I'll ever have dependents that aren't going to leave fur on the couch, that question is still years off for me. In the meantime, you can find me playing "fun aunt" to my friend's dogs (and kids), and checking in on my furry dogchildren, celebrating when they all find safe and happy homes. With carpeted floors, of course.

Surrogate Dog
Caroline Knapp

♡ About six months after she got her puppy, an irrepressible malamute named Oakley, my friend Grace had lunch with a friend on Newbury Street, a chic stretch of restaurants and shops in Boston's Back Bay. Grace, who's about as in love with her dog as a person can be, brought along some pictures of Oakley, and when she pulled them out of her purse to show them, her friend pulled back from the table ever so slightly. "Oh, Grace," she said, raising an eyebrow. "Retreating into the world of furry animals."

Grace told me this story while we were walking in a stretch of conservation land about twenty minutes west of Boston. We'd stopped for a moment at the bank of a pond, and the dogs were engaged in a furious chase along the sand, darting up one side and tearing back, about as happy as dogs get. The sky was steely gray, the air and water calm, and we'd been out walking for about an hour, talking about dogs and the choices in life they help clarify. I remember that Grace stood there with her back to the reservoir and swept one arm out across the scenery. "*This* is retreating?"

Grace and I are both the kind of people that others have in mind when they talk about the tendency among some humans to use dogs as surrogates, to "retreat" into the world of animals in order to bypass more problematic and complex human relationships. I can see the thinking behind this view: Grace and I are both single women who live alone, work out of our homes, invest extraordinary amounts of time and energy in our dogs. We are both prone to periods of isolation and withdrawal, people who might very well prefer lounging around at home with the dog to hanging out at some swank café on Newbury Street. Neither of us has kids. And me, I've left this seven-year relationship with a genuinely good man to spend most evenings holed up in my living room, the dog at my feet. So it's not hard to see why we'd be looked at a bit warily: At least superficially, we appear to have made a rather deliberate set of choices—dogs instead of people, dogs instead of children, dogs instead of men.

And yet there we were, two women intimately engaged in conversation, sharing time and the natural world and our mutual love of animals. Grace, whom I met right around the time I separated from Michael, is a woman of uncommon intelligence and depth, and I doubt our paths even would have crossed had it not been for the dogs: We share the same dog trainer, went to the same dog camp in Vermont, fell into the whole dog world at roughly the same time. In the two years since we met, we've racked up countless hours together in those same woods, and our walks together have become one of the most sustaining aspects of my life, weekly shots to the soul of connection and laughter. We are very much on the same road out there, both of us going it alone in the world, trying to chart courses for ourselves that feel meaningful and true, and aware of the extent to which both our dogs and friendship with each other have factored into that effort. Like she said, *This* is a retreat?

As a culture, we're a bit schizophrenic when it comes to loving dogs, both accepting and suspect. On the positive side, keeping a pet—particularly a dog—can grant you a stamp of normalcy, give you a casual but handy entrée into the social world. A well-known study by New York psychologist Randall Lockwood suggests, almost without exception, that people in the company of a dog are more likely to be regarded by others as friendlier, happier, more relaxed, and less threatening than people who are dogless; in an oft-cited study on the social effects of keeping a dog, British zoologist Peter Messent found that dog walkers in public parks and gardens had higher numbers of positive interactions and more extensive conversations with others than people who were either on their own or with small children.

And yet some fine line exists between "normal" love for a dog and "excessive" love. Care for the dog too much—dote on the dog, spend too much time with the dog, get too attached to the dog—and you get branded as something very different: You're eccentric, or antisocial; you get laughed at. In his book *In the Company of Animals,* James Serpell traces part of what he sees as the cultural denigration of pet-keeping to the popular press, which seems to devote as much space to pet-human relationships as it does to people's sex lives, with the bulk of the coverage designed to highlight the extremes to which today's pet owner goes. There are stories about pet cemeteries and pet summer camps; stories about the modern accessorized dog, with his gold choke chain and Burberry raincoat and special-ordered, hydrant-shaped birthday cake; stories about excess. A classic example, the kind of story the media love to laugh at: Countess Carlotta Liebenstein, an eccentric German noblewoman, who left an estate valued at $80 million to a German shepherd dog called Gunther. The overt message is clear—people who love animals are wacky—but behind it is a more covert and subtle one, a belief, as Serpell describes it, "that pets are no more than substitutes for so-called 'normal' human relationships."

In fact, very little evidence exists to suggest that people with deep attachments to their animals are any weirder than people who are less attached, or that they're focusing an unhealthy degree of social energy on their pets. If anything, dogs tend to widen, rather than narrow, one's social world. "Morgen finds it easier than I ever did to go up to strangers and introduce himself," says Bill, of his three-year-old dachshund. Single and in his fifties, Bill has lived in a high-rise condo in Washington, D.C., for more than ten years. Pre-dog, he hardly knew any of his neighbors; now he knows dozens of them, Morgen having wagged his way into a vastly expanded circle. Pre-dog, Bill led an active social life; today it's doubled: He chairs his condo association's pet committee; his friends' children, who love Morgen, make regular playdates with him and the dog; several of the acquaintanceships he's made through Morgen have blossomed into close friendships, particularly with other dog owners.

This is a classic story: Dog gets owner out of the house, tugs him or her toward new people, expands the human pack. Lisa, a school administrator who owns a small black dachshund mix named Franny, first met Mimi, a social worker who owns a small black miniature poodle named Marty, through a dog group; their dogs became playmates, the women became intimates; when Mimi became pregnant eighteen months later, Lisa became her labor coach. Jonathan, who owns a basenji named Toby, met his current lover, a veterinarian named Mike, through the dog. Dog love became human love, colliding at key points (on their third date Mike turned to him and said, "Jonathan, I really love being with you, but I've gotta ask you to stop bringing me Toby's stool samples"). Like Bill's dachshund, Jonathan's dog gave him a sense of belonging in the world. "I walk with this whole network of people who own dogs," he says, "and I've found this really wonderful community. We all walk our dogs in the morning and the evening, and sometimes I see them in other places, and we call each other by our dogs' names: 'Oh, there's Toby's father, there's Astro's father.'"

Such stories confirm what researchers have documented many times over: Dogs are excellent social lubricants, and they tend to attract relatively social people. Psychologists at the University of Oklahoma have found that people with affectionate attitudes toward their dogs have proportionately affectionate attitudes toward people; British researchers have reported that people who interact frequently with their dogs have a higher desire for affiliation with other people than non–dog owners; a California study reported that elderly pet owners were more self-sufficient, dependable, helpful, optimistic, and socially confident than non–pet owners.

I suppose the key in human-dog relationships—at least as others see them—is degree. Certainly the world feels like a more comfortable, social place to me when I have Lucille by my side: Passersby smile, sometimes stopping to ask a dog question or two; I tend to feel more relaxed and less anonymous when she's with me, and also more approachable, my four-legged ice-breaker at the end of the leash. And yet I'm also aware of that fine line, that question of excess, that view of what's "normal" and what's not. The dog clearly does not occupy a secondary or neatly compartmentalized role in my life, so little seeds of doubt periodically crop up inside: I seem to love this dog too much; is this a problem?

On Christmas Day two years ago, I showed up at my aunt's house for the afternoon, Lucille in tow along with a big bag of Lucille's stuff: a blanket for her to lie on, a couple of chew toys, a big old rawhide bone for her to gnaw while we ate Christmas dinner. I felt a little silly lugging in all that gear—it felt like the canine version of a diaper bag—so I kind of tucked the bag under my arm, then walked into the living room and looked around.

Christmas is a lonely time for me, particularly since my parents' deaths. What is family? Who in the world do I really feel connected to? All those dark existential holiday questions bubble up, and they do so with particular intensity in the aftermath of those losses. I've spent every Christmas since childhood with my aunt and her family, but it's not a group I see much of between holidays, and I remember standing at the entrance to the living room feeling orphaned in the truest sense, as though I were about to spend Christmas with a large group of people who didn't really know me very well. So I hovered for a minute, and then homed in on my cousin Suzanne and her husband, Bill, who'd gotten a puppy right around the time I got Lucille, a standard poodle named Pepper.

Oh, good, I thought. *Common ground.* We said hello and exchanged brief pleasantries, and then I asked Bill, "So how's Pepper?"

Dogs are one of the few subjects I can get truly gabby about, so I think I hoped we'd launch into dog talk from there, trade stories about training and behavior problems and care and feeding. But Bill paused just slightly and said, "Oh . . . um, she's fine. She's turned into a really sweet dog." Then he gave me a kind of blank look, as if to say, "Next question?" and I remember being struck by a sense of acute awkwardness, standing there with my dog and my dog gear and my dog question. Here I am: Dog, dog, dog.

Suzanne and Bill, both physicians, have two young daughters, and they lead very busy lives, and although I'm sure they're very attached to Pepper and are pleased that they got her, she does not occupy a primary role in their world. By contrast, I'd spent the whole day absorbed in my dog—we'd gone for a three-hour hike in the woods that morning, and I'd carted her along with me to Christmas dinner as though she were my daughter or my date, and I felt hugely exposed for a second, as though I was revealing some fundamental difference between me and other people: woman with dog versus man with family. Woman with tiny narrow life versus man with big full life. Woman with bizarre priorities versus man with normal priorities. What's wrong with this picture?

This brand of self-consciousness can hit people who love their dogs deeply, even when they're together with like-minded dog devotees. I was hanging out at a park recently with a woman named Catherine, who owns a yellow Lab named Bailey, and a teenage girl named Katie, who owns a golden retriever/Lab mix named Sadie. At one point Catherine pulled out a little container of treats from her knapsack, then turned to the dogs, who were milling around the picnic table where we sat, and said, "Okay! Who wants a snicky-snack? Would anyone want a snicky-snack?" Her voice was squeaky and high, as though she were addressing a flock of schoolchildren, and hearing herself, she looked at Katie and me and rolled her eyes. "Oh my God," she said. "What is wrong with me?" We just laughed; happens all the time.

And it does happen all the time. Like a lot of dog owners, I have about fifty different terms of endearment for Lucille—sweet pea, and Miss Pea, and pea pod, and peanut, and Miss Peanut—and every once in a while I'll hear myself in the house cooing at her in an overenthused soprano, "Oh, hello, you sweet, sweet pea! Are you the cutest pea there ever was?" and I'll just pray my neighbors can't overhear me, I sound like such a goon. Or I'll be making her dinner, and I'll catch myself imploring her to eat as though she's a toddler—"I have a *delicious* supper for you, Miss Pea! Have a bite of this delicious supper!"—and I'll shake my head: Good Lord, I have gone off the deep end at last. I'm alone with the dog, and I'm alone with her a lot, and so the question of substitution looms large and often: What am I doing here? *Is* she a surrogate for other relationships? *Should* I be investing all this energy elsewhere?

Should: That's the key question, the same one that generated the sense of exposure I felt at Christmas. Should I be living this kind of life or some other kind of life? Should I follow a more traditional path, pursue more traditional goals, let go of that leash and follow not the dog but, like my cousin and her husband, a life that includes marriage, kids, a home with actual people in it? And if I don't follow that path, does that mean there's something wrong with me?

I have been pondering these questions almost since the day I got Lucille, and I'll no doubt continue to wrestle with them over time. On bad days, days when I'm lonely and my world feels small and unproductive and gray, I lean toward the pathologizing view, look around and see myself as some sort of reclusive, dog-obsessed misfit, too fearful and damaged to lead a "real" life. But other times I'm less sure of that. Alongside the seeds of doubt I felt cropping up at Christmas, there was also a small seed of certainty: This dog is an enormous solace to me, a constant companion and witness to my daily life, a being I have come to feel closer to in many ways than members of my own family. She represents a choice, a style of living and loving that may not be conventional but that is valid in its own right, if only because it's my own.

Acknowledgments

It was an honor to work with such a cool and talented group of writers for this collection. Special thanks to friends Dimity McDowell and Abby Mims, who not only wrote outstanding stories that made me proud to know them, but also edited my essay with skill. Thanks, dudes.

Huge thanks to friends, colleagues, and friends-and-colleagues-of-friends-and-colleagues who graciously agreed to lend their writing talents: Robin Troy, Alyssa Shaffer, Tish Hamilton, Tracy Teare, Tricia O'Brien, Katie Arnold, Margaret Littman, Rebecca Skloot, and Maria Goodavage.

To our bold names of the bunch, thank you to Pam Houston, Susan Cheever, Marion Winik, and Sara Corbett for your time and enthusiasm.

Of course, a high-five to Seal Press editor Marisa Solís for suggesting me to head up this project in the first place, and to *my* editor at Seal, Jill Rothenberg, for putting up with all my questions and walking me through every step of this process. It's certainly been real.

Finally, a shout out to Eric, for humoring me through many emailed dog pictures, weekend trips to the Oregon Humane Society, and my general obsession with All Things Dog while working on this book.

About the Contributors

Katie Arnold is the managing editor of *Outside* magazine. She lives in Santa Fe, New Mexico, and writes frequently for *Outside*, *Santa Fean*, and other publications.

Susan Cheever is the author of five novels and six nonfiction books, and has written essays, book reviews, and articles for many magazines and newspapers including *The New Yorker*, *The New York Times*, *Talk*, and *The Washington Post*. She is a former columnist for *Newsday*, writing on everything from parenting to politics, and is currently at work on a book about Concord, Massachusetts, in the 19th century: a biography of the Alcotts, Thoreau, the Emersons, and Hawthorne due in 2006 and entitled *Outbreak of Genius*. She lives in New York City, where she is a professor at the New School University MFA program.

Melinda J. Combs' fiction and nonfiction has appeared in *Far From Home: Father-Daughter Travel Adventures, .ISM Quarterly, Cleansheets.com, Orange Coast Magazine*, and other journals. She also teaches at a variety of schools, including Orange County High School of the Arts. While earning her MA and MFA from Chapman University, she won first place in fiction and nonfiction for the university's journal, *Calliope*. She lives in Huntington Beach, California.

Sara Corbett is a contributing writer at *The New York Times Magazine* and a writer at large for *Runner's World*, where her essay first appeared. Her work has appeared in numerous national magazines, including *Esquire, Outside, Elle*, and *Mother Jones*. She lives in Portland, Maine.

Julia Fulton is an adjunct professor at the University of California at San Diego, teaching in the theatre and literature departments. Her acting experience includes starring roles in TV movies such as *The Challenger* (with Barry Bostwick), *Unholy Matrimony* (with Patrick Duffy), *My Brother's Keeper* (with John Lithgow), plus regular and recurring roles on *ER, Buffy the Vampire Slayer*, and *Melrose Place*, among others.

Maria Goodavage is a former *USA Today* correspondent and author of *The Dog Lover's Companion to California* (www .caldogtravel.com) and two other popular dog books. She also wrote and coproduced an award-winning children's video, *Here's Looking at You, Kid!* (www.funkidsvideo.com), which stars her previous dog, Joe, in the role of, yes, a talking dog. (Unlike Jake, Joe was lucky enough to have Ed Asner portray his voice.) Maria lives in San Francisco with her husband, daughter, and occasionally talkative dog.

Tish Hamilton lives with her husband, baby, and two Great Danes in what she calls a "giant, heated doghouse" in Bernardsville, New Jersey. Her writing has appeared in *Rolling Stone, Sports Illustrated Women*, and *Outside* magazines. She is an executive editor at *Runner's World*.

Pam Houston is the author of two collections of linked short stories, *Cowboys Are My Weakness* and *Waltzing the Cat*. Her stories have been selected for volumes of *Best American Short Stories, The O. Henry Awards, The Pushcart Prize*, and *Best American Short Stories of the Century*. A collection of essays, *A Little More About Me*, was published in the fall of 1999. In 2001 she completed a stage play called *Tracking the Pleiades* and her first novel, *Sighthound,* was published in January 2005. She is the director of creative writing at the University of California at Davis, and she divides her time between Davis, California, and her ranch at 9,000 feet in Colorado near the headwaters of the Rio Grande.

Gail Hulnick is a writer and former radio and TV broadcaster who has published articles about education, health, the arts, and business in such magazines as *Reader's Digest, InFlight,* and *Alive.* She also writes screenplays, novels, and short stories, and is on the lookout for her next canine best friend. She lives in Vancouver, B.C.

Caroline Knapp is the author of *Drinking: A Love Story, Alice K's Guide to Life,* and the *New York Times* bestseller *Pack of Two,* from which this essay was excerpted. She was a contributing editor at *New Woman* magazine and regular columnist for the *Boston Phoenix,* and her work appeared in *Mademoiselle* and *The New York Times.* She died in 2002 at the age of forty-two.

Susan T. Lennon is a freelance writer whose work has appeared in *Newsweek, The Washington Post, USA Weekend* magazine, *Health,* and others. She works from home with Harley and his "brothers," Labrador Ralph and bossy cat Atticus. She and her husband live in Rocky Hill, Connecticut. Her website is www.susanlennon.com

Margaret Littman is a Chicago-based writer who spends part of each day removing dog hair from her keyboard. Her work has appeared in *Wine Enthusiast, Time Out Chicago, Woman's Day, Art & Antiques,* and many other publications. She is the author of *VegOut Vegetarian Guide to Chicago.* She and her spaniel, Natasha, are updating their guidebook, *The Dog Lover's Companion to Chicago,* while debating moving to a climate where they can garden more than four months a year.

Dimity McDowell is a freelance writer who specializes in stories about sports and fitness; she's climbed Mount Kilimanjaro, trekked through the jungles of Borneo and jumped out of an airplane all for the sake of a good story. She's currently the gear editor for *Shape* and a contributing editor at *Health* and *Budget Living.* She lives in Santa Fe, New Mexico.

Abby Mims still lives in Portland, Oregon, but she is happy to report that she no longer resides with her parents. She is at work on a collection of short stories and a memoir about her sister's battle with cancer that (among other things) highlights the various neuroses of her family members—including herself. A graduate of the University of California at Irvine MFA program, her work has been published in *The Santa Monica Review, Swink, Other Voices,* and *Women on the Edge: West Coast Women Write.*

Tricia O'Brien lives with Lyle in New York City, where they go for daily play sessions and frequent runs in Central Park. The features editor for *American Baby* magazine, she has also worked as an editor for *Healthy Living, Natural Health,* and www.prevention .com. Her articles have appeared in magazines such as *Fitness, Shape, Prevention, Seattle, Family Circle, Ladies' Home Journal,* and *Parents.*

After a career as an advertising copy and scriptwriter for national corporate accounts, Kathryn Renner now focuses on writing for national and regional magazines. She specializes in profile, home, and lifestyle stories. Her essays have appeared in *The Christian Science Monitor,* the *Chicago Tribune, Country Home, Home Companion, Victoria, Horizon Air* magazine, and others. She lives in Seattle.

Jill Rothenberg is a senior editor at Seal Press. As a former news reporter and photographer, she was always on the lookout for stories with a canine angle. A dog mom in spirit to Dave's weimaraner, Olive, and a doting aunt to her friends' dogs, she lives in Oakland, California.

Jennifer Sexton lives in Cape Cod with her husband, two-year-old daughter, a lop-eared rabbit, a twenty-year-old cockatiel, and two parakeets, but no dog. Yet. Her work has appeared in the Seal Press anthology *Italy, a Love Story,* as well as in *VIA* magazine, *Synapse, Women's Work, Redheaded Stepchild,* and *4th Street Press.*

Alyssa Shaffer is the fitness director for *Fitness* magazine and has written numerous health and fitness articles for such publications as *Cooking Light, Men's Journal, Tennis,* and *Shape.* She lives and works in New York City, where she spends lots of time walking in the park with her entire family: Scott, Nolan, Layla, and Jett.

Sarah Shey has written for *The New York Times, Time Out New York, Bridal Guide,* the *Philadelphia Inquirer, This Old House* magazine, the *Des Moines Register, The Iowan,* and *The Christian Science Monitor.* She received her MFA in writing from Columbia University and her BA from Northwestern University. Shey wrote the children's book *Sky All Around* and is currently at work on a nonfiction narrative. She lives in Brooklyn, New York.

Rebecca Skloot is a New York City–based freelance writer, a contributing editor at *Popular Science* magazine, and a television correspondent for PBS's *Nova scienceNOW* series. She writes for *The New York Times, The New York Times Magazine,* and *Discover* magazine, among others. Her work has been anthologized in several textbooks and essay collections, including *The Best Food Writing 2005.* Her first book, *The Immortal Life of Henrietta Lacks,* is forthcoming from Crown. Her website is www.rebeccaskloot.com.

Tracy Teare is a Falmouth, Maine–based freelance writer who specializes in fitness and health. Coauthor of *Walking Through Pregnancy and Beyond* and a former contributing editor at *Shape,* Tracy's work has also been published in *Glamour, Self, Fitness, Health, Cooking Light,* and *Fit Pregnancy.*

Abigail Thomas lives in Woodstock, New York. Her fifth book, *A Three Dog Life,* will be published in 2006. Her previous books are *Safekeeping,* a memoir, *An Actual Life,* a novel, and two story collections, *Getting Over Tom* and *Herb's Pajamas.*

Robin Troy teaches fiction writing at Southern Connecticut State University in New Haven. She received her MFA in fiction from the University of Montana in Missoula, where she was also a staff writer for the *Missoula Independent* newspaper. Her first novel, *Floating,* was published in 1998.

Before joining the copy department at *Sunset* magazine, Lisa Vollmer worked as a freelance writer and editor, specializing in finance and business topics. She authored three career guides for San Francisco–based publisher WetFeet Press, including *Job Hunting in the San Francisco Bay Area* and *Beat the Street II: an Investment Banking Interview Practice Guide.* More recently, her work has been published in *Sunset, Living 101* (also published by Sunset), and *Stanford Business* magazine. She lives in Menlo Park, California, with her husband, Brian.

Since 1991, Marion Winik has been a regular commentator on National Public Radio's *All Things Considered.* She is the author of four books of creative nonfiction, among them *First Comes Love,* a memoir of her marriage, *Telling,* a best-selling collection of personal essays, and *The Lunch-Box Chronicles* and *Rules for the Unruly.* Her collection of essays, *Above Us Only Sky,* was published by Seal Press in 2005. Her essays and articles have been published in *O, Salon, Travel+Leisure, National Geographic Traveler, Texas Monthly, Men's Journal, Reader's Digest, Utne, Health, Cooking Light, Redbook,* and *More,* among others. She lives in Glen Rock, Pennsylvania, with her husband and their five children.

About the Editor

Megan McMorris is the author of *Oregon Hiking* and coauthor of *Pacific Northwest Hiking*. Her magazine articles have appeared in *Fitness, Self, Cooking Light, Runner's World,* and *Glamour,* among others. She lives in Portland, Oregon, where she's currently working on a guidebook to her city; *Moon Handbooks Portland* will be published in 2007. Her website is www.meganmcmorris.com.

THE DOG LOVER'S COMPANION

A special breed of guidebook for travelers and residents who don't want to leave their canine pals behind.

INSIDER INFORMATION on hundreds of off-leash areas, parks, hiking trails, camping areas, and beaches, all rated from a pooch's perspective on a one- to four-paw scale • **CANINE COVERAGE** of dog-friendly hotels, restaurants, and shops, plus tips on pup safety and etiquette • **DOGGY DIVERSIONS**, such as ferry trips, train rides, winery visits, and pet parades • **DETAILED MAPS** and driving directions for easy travel planning.

THE DOG LOVER'S COMPANION GUIDES ARE AVAILABLE FOR:

THE BAY AREA

BOSTON

CALIFORNIA

CHICAGO

FLORIDA

LOS ANGELES

WWW.DOGLOVERSCOMPANION.COM

NEW ENGLAND

NEW YORK CITY

THE PACIFIC NORTHWEST

PHILADELPHIA

WASHINGTON D.C.

AVAILABLE AT BOOKSTORES AND THROUGH ONLINE BOOKSELLERS

Selected titles from Seal Press

For more than twenty-five years, Seal Press has published groundbreaking books. By women. For women. Visit our website at www.sealpress.com.

Es Cuba: Life and Love on an Illegal Island by Lea Aschkenas. $15.95. 1-58005-179-0. This triumphant love story captures a beautiful and intangible sense of sadness and admiration for the country of Cuba and for its people.

Reckless: The Outrageous Lives of Nine Kick-Ass Women by Gloria Mattioni. $14.95. 1-58005-148-0. From Lisa Distefano, former *Playboy* model who captains a pirate vessel on her quest to protect sea life, to Libby Riddles, the first woman to win the legendary Iditarod, this collection of profiles explores the lives of nine women who took unconventional life paths to achieve extraordinary results.

The Risks of Sunbathing Topless: And Other Funny Stories from the Road edited by Kate Chynoweth. $15.95. 1-58005-141-3. From Kandahar to Baja to Moscow, these wry, amusing essays capture the comic essence of bad travel, and the female experience on the road.

Mexico, A Love Story: Women Write about the Mexican Experience edited by Camille Cusumano. $15.95. 1-58005-156-1. In this rich anthology, two dozen women describe the country they love and why they have fallen under its spell.

Tied in Knots: Funny Stories from the Wedding Day edited by Lisa Taggart and Samantha Schoech. $14.05 1-58005-175-8. Twenty witty women will have you in stitches as they describe wild, embarrassing, and unexpected moments leading up to the Big Day.